HELLO KITTY
World Atlas

Hello Kitty World Atlas

Collins
An imprint of HarperCollins Publishers
Westerhill Road
Bishopbriggs
Glasgow
G64 2QT

Maps © CollinsBartholomew Ltd 2013
© 1976, 2013 Sanrio Co., Ltd

First published 2013

ISBN 978-0-00-752360-3
ISBN 978-0-00-752944-5

Imp 001

The contents of this edition of Collins Hello Kitty World Atlas are believed
correct at the time of printing. Nevertheless the publishers can accept no
responsibility for errors or omissions, changes in the detail given, or for
any expense or loss thereby caused.

British Library Cataloguing in Publication Data. A catalogue record for
this book is available from the British Library.

Printed and bound in Hong Kong   Design ©HarperCollins Publishers

All mapping in this atlas is generated from Collins Bartholomew digital
databases. Collins Bartholomew, the UK's leading independent
geographical information supplier, can provide a digital, custom,
and premium mapping service to a variety of markets.

visit our websites at:

www.collins.co.uk
www.collinseducation.com
www.collinsbartholomew.com

HELLO KITTY
World Atlas

Contents

An atlas is a book of maps. Take a journey around the world with this atlas. It is divided up into continents and regions. Some of the bigger countries even have a whole map themselves. Use the atlas to see where different countries in the world are. See which ones are large and which ones are small, which countries join up with others and which ones are islands all by themselves.

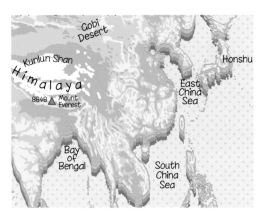

World maps

The first few pages show maps of the whole world and from these you can learn where every country is and where the major physical features are. You can find out even more about these places by searching through the continents and regions mapped in the rest of the atlas.

Maps of each continent

All of the maps are grouped into continental sections depending on where they are in the world. Some of the Oceans are also mapped and are shown within the continents that they border. Each section starts with a map of the whole continent and includes some interesting facts about that particular continent, such as its highest point, or largest lake.

Reference maps

Most of the pages in an atlas are made up of reference maps. These are maps which zoom in and look more closely at specific areas of the world. In this atlas the reference maps typically show a few countries at once. This can be great for comparing countries with their neighbours, learning which ones share borders, seeing the shapes of the countries, and seeing where the major cities are located.

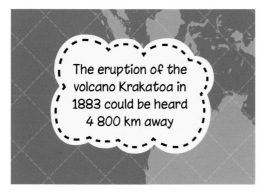

> The eruption of the volcano Krakatoa in 1883 could be heard 4 800 km away

Country facts and flags

Every country in the world is different. This section of the atlas shows you the country's flag, the name of its capital city, its population and the area it takes up on the earth's surface.

Amazing facts

Towards the back of the book there are some maps which show a selection of interesting geographical facts. Many of these facts are the kinds you would expect to find in an atlas, like the highest mountain in the world, but there are also some surprises in there.

Argentina

Buenos Aires

40 765 000

2 766 889 sq km

Index

The very back of the book is an index to all of the places shown on the reference maps. If places are shown more than once, the index lists where they appear in the most detail.

North
America

Europe

Africa

South
America

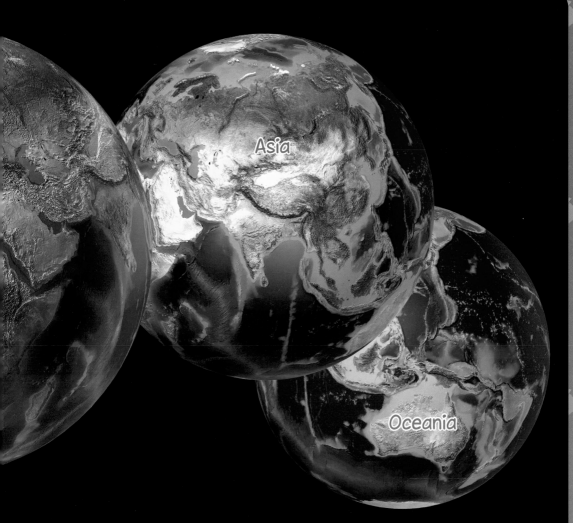

Asia

Oceania

The world refers to the place where we live. Its proper name is the planet Earth. The Earth is spherical which means you can only ever see part of it at once. Its surface is made up of a mixture of land areas and water areas. The land areas are called continents and the water areas are called Oceans and Seas. There are 7 continents in total. They are called South America, North America, Europe, Africa, Asia, Oceania and Antarctica.

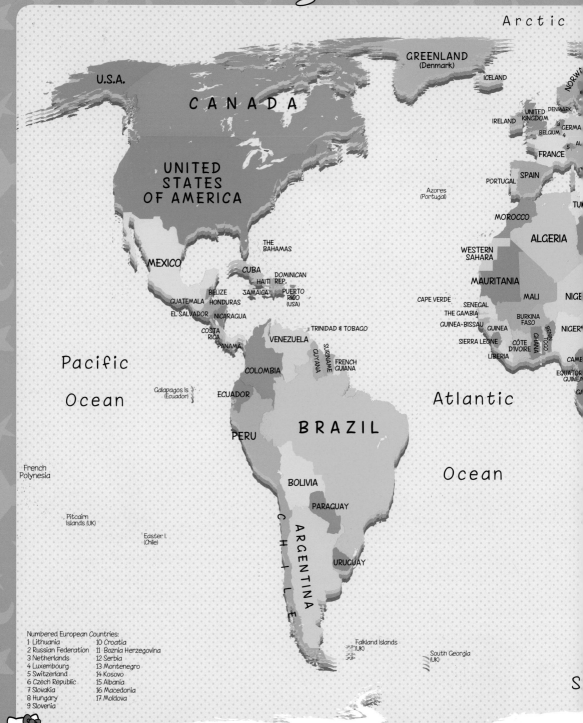

Arctic

GREENLAND
(Denmark)

ICELAND

NORWA

U.S.A.

C A N A D A

IRELAND | UNITED | DENMARK
KINGDOM
BELGIUM | 3 | GERMA
4
5 | AL

FRANCE

UNITED
STATES
OF AMERICA

PORTUGAL | SPAIN

Azores
(Portugal)

MOROCCO

ALGERIA

TU

WESTERN
SAHARA

THE
BAHAMAS

MEXICO

MAURITANIA

MALI

NIGE

CUBA
HAITI | DOMINICAN
REP.

BELIZE | JAMAICA | PUERTO
RICO
(USA)

CAPE VERDE

SENEGAL
THE GAMBIA

BURKINA
FASO

NIGER

GUATEMALA | HONDURAS

GUINEA-BISSAU

BENIN

HONDURAS

GUINEA

TOGO

GHANA

EL SALVADOR | NICARAGUA

SIERRA LEONE

CÔTE
D'IVOIRE

CAME

COSTA
RICA

TRINIDAD & TOBAGO

LIBERIA

EQUATOR
GUINEA

PANAMA

VENEZUELA

GA

Pacific

COLOMBIA

GUYANA

SURINAME

FRENCH
GUIANA

Atlantic

Galapagos Is
(Ecuador)

ECUADOR

Ocean

PERU

B R A Z I L

Ocean

French
Polynesia

BOLIVIA

Pitcairn
Islands (UK)

PARAGUAY

Easter I.
(Chile)

C
H
I
L
E

A
R
G
E
N
T
I
N
A

URUGUAY

Falkland Islands
(UK)

South Georgia
(UK)

S

Numbered European Countries:
1 Lithuania   10 Croatia
2 Russian Federation 11 Bosnia Herzegovina
3 Netherlands   12 Serbia
4 Luxembourg   13 Montenegro
5 Switzerland   14 Kosovo
6 Czech Republic   15 Albania
7 Slovakia   16 Macedonia
8 Hungary   17 Moldova
9 Slovenia

cean

RUSSIAN FEDERATION

ONIA
ARUS
UKRAINE
17
ANIA
LGARIA
ECE   TURKEY
CYPRUS
LEBANON
ISRAEL

KAZAKHSTAN

UZBEKISTAN
GEORGIA
ARMENIA AZERBAIJAN
TURKMENISTAN

SYRIA
IRAQ   IRAN
JORDAN
KUWAIT

EGYPT   SAUDI
BAHRAIN
QATAR
UNITED
ARAB
EMIRATES
ARABIA   OMAN

SUDAN   ERITREA   YEMEN

DJIBOUTI

NTRAL
RICAN
PUBLIC

SOUTH
SUDAN   ETHIOPIA

SOMALIA

MOCRATIC
EPUBLIC
OF THE
CONGO

UGANDA
KENYA

RWANDA
BURUNDI
TANZANIA

KYRGYZSTAN

TAJIKISTAN

AFGHAN-
ISTAN

PAKISTAN

NEPAL   BHUTAN

BANGLA-
DESH

INDIA   MYANMAR
(BURMA)

THAILAND

SRI
LANKA

MALDIVES

SEYCHELLES

MONGOLIA

CHINA

N. KOREA
S. KOREA   JAPAN

TAIWAN

LAOS

VIETNAM

CAMBODIA

PHILIPPINES

BRUNEI
MALAYSIA

SINGAPORE

INDONESIA

EAST
TIMOR

Pacific
Ocean

Northern
Mariana Is.
(USA)

MARSHALL
ISLANDS

PALAU

FED. STATES OF
MICRONESIA

NAURU

PAPUA
NEW
GUINEA

SOLOMON
ISLANDS

VANUATU

New
Caledonia
(Fr.)

Indian
Ocean

A

ZAMBIA
ZIMBABWE

MALAWI

MOZAMBIQUE

COMOROS

MADAGASCAR

MAURITIUS

OTSWANA

SWAZILAND

P. OF
UTH
RICA   LESOTHO

AUSTRALIA

NEW
ZEALAND

Îles Kerguelen
(Fr.)

thern Ocean

ANTARCTICA

Arctic

Greenland

Baffin
Bay

Iceland

Bering
Sea

Mount
McKinley
6194

Hudson
Bay

British
Isles

North
Sea

NORTH

Newfoundland

Mont Blanc
4810

Alps

AMERICA

Appalachian Mts

Medit

Atlantic

S a h

Sierra Madre

Gulf of
Mexico

Caribbean
Sea

Ocean

Galapagos
Islands

Amazon
Basin

SOUTH

Pacific

AMERICA

Lake
Titicaca

Ocean

A
n
d
e
s

Aconcagua
6959

Cape
Good H

Patagonia

Falkland
Islands

Sout

Cape Horn

Weddell
Sea

Arctic
Ocean

GREENLAND
(Denmark)

Bering
Sea

Baffin
Bay

ALASKA
(U.S.A.)

Mount
McKinley △

Baffin Island

Nuuk□

Anchorage

Iqaluit

Hudson
Bay

CANADA

Edmonton

Calgary

Québec

Vancouver

Montréal

Seattle

Winnipeg

Ottawa□

Boston

Portland

Lake
Superior

Toronto

Minneapolis-
St Paul

Detroit

New York

R. Missouri

Chicago

San
Francisco

Denver

Kansas
City

St Louis

Pittsburgh

Washington D.

UNITED STATES
OF AMERICA

Los Angeles
San Diego

Atlanta

Phoenix

Dallas

El Paso

R. Mississippi

THE
BAHAM

Houston

New
Orleans

Miami

Nassau

Pacific

Monterrey

Gulf of
Mexico

Havana□

CUBA

Port-e
Prir

Ocean

MEXICO

JAMAICA
Kingston

Guadalajara

Caribbe

Mexico City□ ○Puebla

BELIZE

Belmopan

HONDURAS

GUATEMALA

Tegucigalpa

Guatemala City□

NICARAGUA

San Salvador

Panama C

EL SALVADOR

Managua
San José

PANAMA

COSTA RICA

North America is the largest continent in the western hemisphere. It is surrounded by great oceans: the Arctic to the north, the Pacific to the west and the Atlantic to the east. The countries of North America are a mixture of the large nations of Canada, USA and Mexico in the north and the tiny Caribbean island nations in the south.

Facts.

Area:
24 680 331 square kilometres
(9 529 129 square miles)

Largest country:
Canada
9 984 670 square kilometres
(3 855 103 square miles)

Longest river:
Mississippi-Missouri
5969 kilometres (3709 miles)

Highest mountain:
Mount McKinley
6194 metres (20 321 feet)

Largest lake:
Lake Superior
82 100 square kilometres
(31 698 square miles)

Largest island:
Greenland
2 175 600 square kilometres
(840 004 square miles)

Atlantic

Ocean

rmuda
(UK)

DOMINICAN
REPUBLIC

ANTIGUA AND
BARBUDA

PUERTO
RICO
(USA)

DOMINICA

San
Juan

BARBADOS

Santo
Domingo

GRENADA

ST LUCIA

TRINIDAD &
TOBAGO

a

ST VINCENT
AND THE
GRENADINES

RUSSIAN FED.

Anadyr

Wrangel Island

ARCT

Chukchi Sea

Bering Strait

Brooks Range

Beaufort Sea

B Isl

Bering Sea

U. S. A.

(Alaska)

Aleutian Islands

Mount McKinley 6194

Fairbanks

Alaska Range

Anchorage

Great Bear Lake

Seward

Gulf of Alaska

Juneau

Whitehorse

Yellowknife

Great S Lake

C

Hay River

A

Rocky

Lake Athabasc

Dawson Creek

Fort McMurra

Grande Prairie

PACIFIC

OCEAN

Prince Rupert

Mountains

Edmonton

Vancouver Island **Vancouver**

Victoria

Calgary

Saskatc

Re

Seattle

Great Pl

Spokane

Lethbridge

Portland

Eugene

Great

Boise

U. S. A.

San Francisco

Sacramento

San Jose

Salt Lake City

Cheyen

CEAN

Queen
Elizabeth
Islands

Parry Islands

Greenland Sea

GREENLAND
(Denmark)

ICELAND

Reykjavik ⌂

Baffin
Bay

Davis Strait

toria
nd

Baffin Island

Foxe
Basin

Nuuk ◇

Iqaluit

Hudson Strait

Labrador
Sea

A   D   A

Churchill

Hudson
Bay

Labrador

Scheffervile

Happy Valley-
Goose Bay

Lake
Winnipeg

Canadian Shield

Sept-Îles

Newfoundland

St John's

Gulf of
St Lawrence

Winnipeg

Thunder Bay

Québec

Moncton

Lake Superior

Sault Sainte Marie

Montréal

Halifax

nneapolis-
St Paul

Duluth

Lake Huron

Ottawa ⌂

Portland

ATLANTIC

Lake Michigan

Toronto

Lake Ontario

Boston

OCEAN

Milwaukee

Detroit

Lake Erie

Providence

Cape Cod

Des Moines

Chicago

Cleveland

New York

PACIFIC OCEAN

Vancouver Island
Victoria
Vancouver
Calgary
Swan River
Cranbrook
Lethbridge
Regina
Winnipeg
Seattle
Olympia
Mount Rainier 4392
Spokane
Shelby
Estevan
Mount St Helens 2550
Great Falls
Williston
Minot
Grand Forks
Portland
Salem
La Grande
Butte
Miles City
Billings
Bismarck
Fargo
Bend
Boise
Idaho Falls
Buffalo
Eureka
Mount Shasta 4317
Klamath Falls
Twin Falls
Casper
Rapid City
Pierre
Sioux Falls
Winnemucca
Green River
Sioux City
Sacramento
Reno
Ely
Great Salt Lake
Salt Lake City
Cheyenne
North Platte
Omaha
San Francisco
Great Basin
San Jose
Fresno
Tonopah
Grand Junction
Denver
Colorado Springs
Junction City
Kansas City
Mount Whitney 4418
Cedar City
Dodge City
Bakersfield
Las Vegas
Colorado Plateau
Wheeler Peak 4011
Los Angeles
Riverside
Flagstaff
Santa Fe
Tulsa
San Diego
Phoenix
Albuquerque
Amarillo
Oklahoma City
Tijuana
Mexicali
Yuma
Tucson
Lubbock
Dallas
Picacho del Diablo 3096
Nogales
El Paso
Fort Worth
Waco
Lázaro Cárdenas
Caborca
Ciudad Juárez
Pecos
Edwards Plateau
Austin
Guadalupe (Mexico)
Hermosillo
Chihuahua
Piedras Negras
Houston
San Antonio
Galveston
Ciudad Obregón
MEXICO
Jiménez
Monclova
Corpus Christi
Los Mochis
Reynosa
Torreón
Monterrey
La Paz
Durango
Ciudad Victoria
Mazatlán

Seattle
Olympia

Coast Ranges
Cascade Range
Sierra Nevada
Bitterroot Range
ROCKY Mountains
Great Plains
UNITED STATES OF AMERICA

Baja California
Gulf of California
Sierra Madre Occidental
Sierra Madre Oriental

CANADA

D A

Moosonee

Matagami

Longlac   Hearst

Thunder
Bay   Val-d'Or   Québec   Presque   Moncton
Lake Superior   Isle   Saint John
              Sault Sainte Marie   Halifax
Marquette   Montréal
                                    Ottawa □   Augusta
Minneapolis-   Portland
St Paul   Traverse
         City   Toronto   L. Ontario   Boston
Green Bay   Hamilton   Rochester   Cape Cod
         Grand   Buffalo   Albany   Providence
Madison   Rapids   Detroit   Hartford
Milwaukee   Toledo   Lake Erie   Erie   New York
                                            Long Island
Chicago   Cleveland
Iowa   Pittsburgh   Philadelphia
City   Columbus   Baltimore
Indianapolis   Dover
                            Washington D.C.
St Louis   Cincinnati   Charleston
                    Richmond   Norfolk
ringfield   ATLANTIC
         Nashville   Knoxville   Raleigh   OCEAN
Memphis   Chattanooga   Charlotte
                    Wilmington
le   Birmingham   Atlanta   Augusta
k   Columbus   Charleston
eport   Jackson   Montgomery
                        Jacksonville
Baton   Mobile   Tallahassee
Rouge
ette   Orlando   Cape
Morgan   New Orleans   Canaveral   Grand
City   Mississippi   Bahama
     Delta   Tampa   Freeport
                        City   THE
                West Palm Beach   BAHAMAS
                    Miami   Nassau □
ulf of Mexico
                            Andros   Turks and
                                    Caicos Islands
                Straits of Florida   (UK)
Havana □   CUBA   Great
                            Inagua

San Diego
Phoenix
Lubbock
Tijuana
Mexicali
Tucson
UNITE
Nogales
El Paso
OF A
Ciudad
Juárez
Pecos
Lázaro
Cárdenas
Caborca
Austin
Guadalupe
(Mexico)
Hermosillo
Chihuahua
San
Antonio
Piedras
Negras
Punta
Eugenia
Ciudad
Obregón
Jiménez
Corpu
Christ
Monclova
Los Mochis
Torreón
Reynosa
Monterrey
La Paz
MEXICO
Durango
Ciudad
Victoria
San José
del Cabo
Mazatlán
Aguascalientes
Ciudad
de Valles
Guadalajara
León
Puerto Vallarta
Querétaro
Islas
Revillagigedo
(Mexico)
Colima
Mexico City
Toluca
Pue
Popocatépetl
5452
Lázaro
Cárdenas
Oaxc
Acapulco
Sierra Madre del S
Puerto Áng

Gulf of California
Baja California
Sierra Madre Occidental
Sierra Madre Oriental

PACIFIC

OCEAN

Little Rock

Atlanta

Birmingham

Augusta

Wilmington

Jackson

Columbus

Charleston

Montgomery

Savannah

Mobile

Lafayette

Jacksonville

Baton Rouge

Houston

New Orleans

Morgan City

Galveston

as

TATES

RICA

A T L A N T I C

O C E A N

Orlando

Tampa

West Palm Beach

Miami

Grand Bahama

Freeport City

Great Abaco

Nassau THE BAHAMAS

G u l f   o f

M e x i c o

Straits of Florida

Andros

Turks and Caicos Islands (UK)

Havana

CUBA

Great Inagua

Grand Turk

Mérida

Cancún

Isla de la Juventud

G r e a t e r

HAITI

Port-au-Prince

Campeche

Campeche

Yucatán

Cayman Islands (UK)

Guantánamo

ruz Bay

Chetumal

Montego Bay

JAMAICA

zacoalcos

Belize

Kingston

A n t i l l e s

Belmopan

Juchitán

BELIZE

C a r i b b e a n

ulf of ntepec

GUATEMALA

San Pedro Sula

HONDURAS

S e a

Guatemala City

Tegucigalpa

San Salvador

EL SALVADOR

San Miguel

NICARAGUA

Managua

Lake Nicaragua

Barranquilla

Cartagena

COSTA RICA

San José

Colón

Chirripó 3819

Panama City

Cúcuta

David

Isthmus of Panama

PANAMA

COLOMBIA

Bucaramanga

Tampa
St Petersburg
U.S.A.

Grand
Bahama

West Palm Beach
Fort Lauderdale
Freeport
City
Miami
Great Abaco

New
Providence **Nassau**
**THE
BAHAMAS**

Cat Island

Andros

Gulf of
Mexico

Straits of Florida

Great Exuma
Long Island

Havana
Matanzas
Pinar del Río
Santa
Clara
Acklir
Island

Guane
CUBA
Great
Inagua

Cancún
Isla de la
Juventud
Camagüey
Holguín

G r e a t e r
Bayamo
Guantánamo

MEXICO
Santiago
de Cuba

Cayman
Islands
(UK)
Montego Bay
Jérémie

JAMAICA
A
n
Kingston

Belmopan
C a r i b b e a n
BELIZE

San Pedro Sula

HONDURAS

Tegucigalpa

San
Miguel
NICARAGUA

Managua
Lake
Nicaragua
Barranquilla
COLOMB

COSTA RICA
Cartagena

A T L A N T I C

O C E A N

Turks and
Caicos Islands
(UK)

rand Turk

ispaniola

de-Paix
Cap-Haïtien   Santiago

ITI   ▲ Pico Duarte
                3175
             **Santo
             Domingo**
rt-au-   □
rince   **DOMINICAN
         REPUBLIC**

l l e s

S e a

Ponce
**San
Juan**
□
**PUERTO
RICO
(USA)**

Virgin Is
(UK)

Virgin Is
(USA)

Leeward Islands

Anguilla (UK)
          St-Martin (Fr.)
Sint
Maarten   Barbuda
(Neth.)
                      **ANTIGUA AND
                       BARBUDA**
**ST KITTS
AND NEVIS**   □ **St John's**
                 Antigua
Montserrat
(UK)   **Guadeloupe
             (Fr.)**

Lesser Antilles

DOMINICA □
Roseau
Martinique
(Fr.)

Castries
ST LUCIA

Kingstown
**ST VINCENT AND
THE GRENADINES**

Windward Islands

BARBADOS
□
Bridgetown

GRENADA □

L e s s e r   A n t i l l e s

Curaçao
(Neth.)

Aruba
(Neth.)

St George's

**TRINIDAD AND
TOBAGO**   Tobago

□ **Port
of Spain**

Trinidad

Coro   Güiria

Caracas   Barcelona

Maracaibo   Maturín

Barquisimeto   **Maracay**
      Valencia
                V E N E Z U E L A

21

Caribbean
Sea

Barranquilla
Maracaibo
Caracas
TRINIDAD
AND TOBAGO
Port of
Spain
VENEZUELA
GUYANA
SURINAME
Georgetown
Paramaribo
FRENCH GUIANA
Cayenne
Medellín
Bogotá
COLOMBIA
Galapagos Islands
(Ecuador)
Quito
ECUADOR
Guayaquil
R. Amazon
Belém
São Luís
Manaus
Fortalez
Iquitos
Trujillo
PERU
Arac
BRAZIL
Salvador
Lima
Lake
Titicaca
Brasília
BOLIVIA
Belo
Horizonte
Arequipa
La Paz
Sucre
Pacific
PARAGUAY
Rio de
Janeiro
São Paulo
Antofagasta
Asunción
Curitiba
Ocean
CHILE
ARGENTINA
Porto
Alegre
Juan Fernandez Islands
(Chile)
URUGUAY
Valparaíso
Aconcagua
Montevideo
Santiago
Buenos
Aires
Concepción
Mar del Plata
Falkland Islands
(UK)
Punta
Arenas
Tierra
del
Fuego
South Georgia
(UK)

22

South America stretches farther south from the equator than all the other continents. The longest mountain range in the world, the Andes, runs the full length of the continent. The Amazon rainforest is the largest in the world. Colourful birds and butterflies, giant snakes, jaguars, monkeys and pumas can all be found in this lush forest. People speak Portuguese in Brazil, but Spanish in other countries.

Natal

ecife

A t l a n t i c

O c e a n

Facts.

Area:
17 815 420 square kilometres
(6 878 572 square miles)

Largest country:
Brazil
8 514 879 square kilometres
(3 287 613 square miles)

Longest river:
Amazon
6 516 kilometres (4 049 miles)

Highest mountain:
Aconcagua
6 959 metres (22 831 feet)

Largest lake:
Lake Titicaca
8 340 square kilometres
(3 220 square miles)

Largest island:
Isla Grande de Tierra del Fuego
47 000 square kilometres
(18 147 square miles)

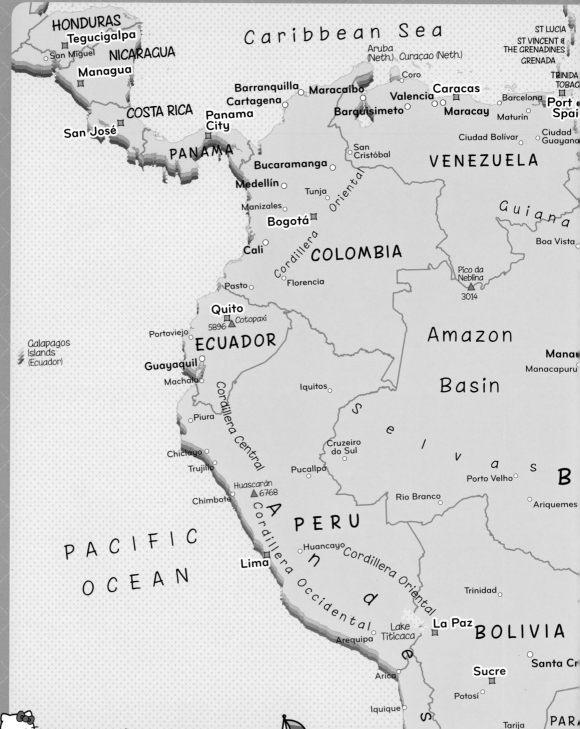

Caribbean Sea

HONDURAS
Tegucigalpa
San Miguel
NICARAGUA
Managua
COSTA RICA
San José
PANAMA
Panama City

Aruba (Neth.) Curaçao (Neth.)
ST LUCIA
ST VINCENT &
THE GRENADINES
GRENADA

Coro
Barranquilla Maracaibo
Cartagena
Barquisimeto
Valencia Caracas
Maracay
Barcelona Port Spai
Maturin
TRINIDA
TOBAG

Bucaramanga
San Cristóbal
VENEZUELA
Ciudad Bolívar Ciudad Guayana

Medellín
Tunja
Manizales
Bogotá
Oriental

Cali
Cordillera
COLOMBIA
Florencia

Guiana

Pasto
Boa Vista
Pico da Neblina
3014

Galapagos Islands (Ecuador)
Quito
Cotopaxi
5896
Portoviejo
ECUADOR
Guayaquil
Machala
Piura

Amazon

Basin

Mana
Manacapuru

Iquitos
Selvas

Cordillera Central

Chiclayo
Trujillo
Chimbote
Huascarán
6768

Cruzeiro do Sul
Pucallpa
Porto Velho
B
Rio Branco
Ariquemes

PACIFIC

OCEAN

A
PERU
Cordillera Occidental
Huancayo
Lima
Cordillera Oriental
n
d
Trinidad
e

Arequipa
Lake Titicaca
La Paz
BOLIVIA
Santa Cr

Arica
Sucre
Potosí

Iquique
Tarija
PARA

24

BADOS

A T L A N T I C
O C E A N

Georgetown

Paramaribo

Cayenne

ANA

SURINAME   FRENCH
            GUIANA

ghlands

Mouths
of the
Amazon

Macapá

Belém

Bragança

Altamira

São Luís

Parnaíba

Itaituba

Fortaleza

Bacabal

Maraba

Teresina

Araguaína

B R A Z I L

Natal

Caruarú

Recife

Petrolina

Maceió

Aracaju

Feira de
Santana

Planalto do
Mato Grosso

B r a z i l i a n

Salvador

Cáceres

Brasília

Itabuna

Rondonópolis

Montes
Claros

Vitória da
Conquista

Goiânia

H i g h l a n d s

Corumbá

Itambé
▲
2033

Uberlândia

Governador Valadares

Campo
Grande

**Belo
Horizonte**

Araçatuba

Barbacena

Vitória

Amazon Basin

S e l v a s

B R A Z I L

Brazilian

Highlands

Petrolina

Araguaina

Maraba

Vitória da
Conquista

Montes
Claros

Itambé
△ 2033

Vitória

Barbacena

Campos

**Rio de
Janeiro**

Belo
Horizonte

Brasília ⌸

Goiânia

Uberlândia

Araraquara

Campinas

**São
Paulo**

Santos

Paranaguá

Florianópolis

Lagoa dos Patos

Maringá

Curitiba

Passo
Fundo

Santa
Maria

**Porto
Alegre**

Uruguaiana

Planalto do
Mato Grosso

Rondonópolis

Cáceres

Corumbá

Campo
Grande

Araçatuba

Dourados

Foz do Iguaçu

PARAGUAY

Gran Chaco

Asunción ◼

Formosa

Corrientes

P A O

Ariquemes

Porto Velho

Trinidad

BOLIVIA

Santa Cruz ○

Sucre ⌸

La Paz ◼

Potosí

Tarija

San Salvador
de Jujuy

Catamarca

La Rioja

Nevado Ojos
del Salado
△ 6908

Rio Branco

Cordillera Oriental

Lake
Titicaca

Arequipa

Arica

Iquique

Antofagasta

Copiapó

Calama

A n d e s

Atacama Desert

PERU

P A O

26

South Georgia
(UK)

ATLANTIC

OCEAN

Montevideo

Mar del Plata

Buenos
Aires

Falkland Islands (UK)
Stanley
East Falkland

West Falkland

Bahía
Blanca

Viedma

Golfo San Matías

Rawson

Comodoro Rivadavia
Golfo de San Jorge

Bahía
Grande

Strait of
Magellan

Tierra del Fuego

Ushuaia

Santa
Rosa

P a m p a

Río
Cuarto

Neuquén

Perito
Moreno

Punta
Arenas

Mendoza

Esquel

Puerto
Natales

Aconcagua
6959

Santiago

Valparaíso

Talca

Concepción

Temuco

Puerto Montt

Isla
de Chiloé

Cerro
San Valentín

4058

F I C   O C E A N

New Guinea

▲ Mount Wilhelm

Lae ○

PAPUA NEW GUINEA

Arafura Sea

Port Moresby □

Great Barrier Reef

Coral Sea

Timor Sea

Darwin ○

Cairns ○

Indian Ocean

Townsville ○

Alice Springs ○

Rockhampton ○

A U S T R A L I A

Lake Eyre

Brisbane ○

Gold Coast ○

R. Darling

Kalgoorlie ○

Newcastle ○

Sydney ○

Great Australian Bight

Adelaide ○

R. Murray

Canberra □

Perth ○

Melbourne ○

Tasm

Geelong ○

Tasmania

Hobart ○

Oceania is the smallest continent and lies within the tropics. It is made up of the countries of Australia, New Zealand, Papua New Guinea and over 20 000 small Pacific islands. Australia is by far the largest country and most of the population live on the coast. The central region of the country is a vast desert known as the outback. New Zealand is mountainous with a temperate climate and Papua New Guinea is mainly rainforest.

☒ Yaren
NAURU

KIRIBATI

**SOLOMON
ISLANDS**

☒ ⸱iara

TUVALU

VANUATU

☒ Port Vila

SAMOA

American
Samoa
(USA)

FIJI

☒ Suva

New
Caledonia
(Fr.)

☒ Nouméa

P a c i f i c

O c e a n

⸱ e a

North
Island

○ Auckland

**NEW
ZEALAND**

Wellington

○ Christchurch

South
Island

○ Dunedin

Facts.

Area:
8 844 516 square kilometres
(3 414 887 square miles)

Largest country:
Australia
7 692 024 square kilometres
(2 969 907 square miles)

Longest river:
Murray-Darling
3750 kilometres (2330 miles)

Largest lake:
Lake Eyre
0-8900 square kilometres
(0-3436 square miles

Largest island:
New Guinea*
808 510 square kilometres
(312 167 square miles)

✳ *half of New Guinea is in Asia

29

Sumba

Timor
Kupang

A r a f u r

Timor Sea

Darwin
Arnh

Katherine

Kimberley
Plateau

Broome

Halls Creek

Tanami Dese

Port
Hedland

Great Sandy Desert

Newman

Macdon

A U S T R

Gibson Desert

Musgrave Ranges

I N D I A N

O C E A N

Great Victoria
Desert

Geraldton

Kalgoorlie

Nullarbor Plain

Perth
Fremantle

Norseman

Great Australia
Bight

Esperance

Albany

Port
Moresby

Honiara

Gulf
of
Carpentaria

Cape
York
Peninsula

Great Barrier Reef

Coral Sea

kly Tableland

Cairns

Townsville

Mount Isa

Mackay

Great Dividing Range

e Springs

Barcaldine

Rockhampton

A L I A

Simpson
Desert

Maryborough

Lake
Eyre

Sturt
Stony
Desert

Toowoomba

Brisbane

Gold Coast

PACIFIC

OCEAN

Dirranbandi

Bourke

Grafton

Flinders Ranges

Port Augusta

Broken
Hill

Dubbo

Port Macquarie

Great Dividing Range

Newcastle

incoln

Adelaide

Hay

Sydney

Wollongong

Kangaroo
Island

Murray Bridge

Wagga
Wagga

Canberra

Horsham

Mount Kosciuszko
2229

Mount Gambier

Melbourne

Geelong

Bairnsdale

Tasman Sea

Burnie

Tasmania

Hobart

PACIFIC

OCEAN

North Island

East Cape

Gisborne

Bay of
Plenty

Napier

Tauranga

Taupo

Whangarei

Manukau

Palmerston
North

Hamilton

Wellington

Auckland

△ Mount Egmont
2518

Cook Str

North Cape

Blenheim

Cape Maria
van Diemen

Tasman
Bay

Nelson

Cape Farewell

Tasman

Sea

NEW
ZEALAND

Chatham Islands
(New Zealand)

Bounty Islands
(New Zealand)

Antipodes Islands
(New Zealand)

S O U T H E R N   O C E A N

South Island

Christchurch

Mount Cook ▲
3754

Timaru

Dunedin

Queenstown

Invercargill

Southern

Stewart Island

Cape
Providence

Auckland Islands
(New Zealand)

Campbell Island
(New Zealand)

A S I A

Beijing

Tokyo

Aleutian Islands

Hawaiia

Manila

Northern
Mariana
Islands
(USA)

MARSHALL
ISLANDS

P A C

Challenger Deep
10920

PALAU

Caroline
Islands

M i c r o n e s i a

Gilbert
Islands

O

A

C

P
o
l
y
n
e

SOLOMON
ISLANDS

M
e
l
a
n
e
s
i
a

TUVALU

Phoenix
Islands

Port
Moresby

Coral
Sea

VANUATU

SAMOA

FIJI

Suva

TONGA

Coo
Islan
(NZ)

New
Caledonia
(Fr.)

I N D I A N
O C E A N

Great Barrier Reef

O C E A N I A

Canberra

T a s m a n
S e a

Wellington

34

NORTH
AMERICA

ATLANTIC
OCEAN

○ Los Angeles

◨ Mexico
City

F   I   C

A   N

◨ Bogotá

Galapagos
Islands
(Ecuador)

Marquesas Islands

Tuamotu Islands

Society Islands

French
Polynesia
(Fr.)

Tubuai Islands

◨ Lima

Pitcairn Islands
(UK)

Easter Island
(Chile)

SOUTH AMERICA

Santiago ◨

...lands

...nolulu

...slands

...a

Arctic Ocean

St Petersburg

Moscow

Perm

Ural Mountains

RUSSIAN FEDERATION

Yakutsk

Chelyabinsk

Omsk

Novosibirsk

Irkutsk

Harbin

Volgograd

Astana

KAZAKHSTAN

Ulan Bator

MONGOLIA

Shenyang

Ankara

TURKEY

GEORGIA

Caspian
Sea

ARMENIA

AZERBAIJAN

UZBEKISTAN

Almaty

Tashkent

Ürümqi

Beijing

Pyongyang

CYPRUS

LEBANON

SYRIA

ISRAEL

TURKMENISTAN

KYRGYZSTAN

Tianjin

JORDAN

Baghdad

Tehran

Ashgabat

TAJIKISTAN

Lanzhou

Xi'an

Nanjing

Shang

IRAQ

KUWAIT

IRAN

Kabul

AFGHANISTAN

Islamabad

CHINA

R. Chang Jiang

Wuhan

Kuwait

Riyadh

BAHRAIN

QATAR

Lahore

Delhi

Himalaya

Chongqing

SAUDI
ARABIA

UNITED
ARAB
EMIRATES

Muscat

PAKISTAN

New
Delhi

NEPAL

Mount
Everest

BHUTAN

Guangzhou

Hong
Kong

San'a

YEMEN

OMAN

Karachi

BANGLADESH

Dhaka

MYANMAR
(BURMA)

Hanoi

VIETNAM

LAOS

Aden

Arabian
Sea

Mumbai

INDIA

Deccan

Kolkata

Nay Pyi Taw

Vientiane

South
China
Sea

Socotra
(Yemen)

Hyderabad

Bay
of
Bengal

Yangon

THAILAND

CAMBODIA

Bangkok

Phnom
Penh

Chennai

Andaman Is
(India)

Ho Chi
Minh City

SRI
LANKA

Nicobar Is
(India)

BRUNEI

Sri Jayewardenepura
Kotte

Colombo

MALAYSIA

MALDIVES

Kuala Lumpur
Putrajaya

SINGAPORE

Borneo

Indian
Ocean

Sumatra

INDONES

Jakarta

Surabaya

Java

Asia is the largest continent. It is bigger than Europe and Africa combined. Asia extends from the Ural mountains to the Pacific Ocean in the east and from the Arctic Ocean to the Indian Ocean in the south. Climates vary from the cold Arctic in the north to hot tropical in the south.

a of
notsk

Sapporo

of   JAPAN
an   Tokyo

Osaka

Pacific
Ocean

on

IPPINES
ila

Mindanao
Davao

New
Guinea

es

akassar

Dili
EAST TIMOR

Facts.

Area:
45 036 492 square kilometres
(17 388 686 square miles)

Largest country:
Russian Federation
17 075 400 square kilometres
(6 592 849 square miles)

Longest river:
Chang Jiang
6380 kilometres (3964 miles)

Highest mountain:
Mount Everest
8848 metres (29 028 feet)

Largest lake:
Caspian Sea
371 000 square kilometres
(143 243 square miles)

Largest island:
Borneo
745 561 square kilometres
(287 863 square miles)

Leshan
Chongqing
Nanchang
Nin

Thimphu
BHUTAN
Dibrugarh
Gongga
Shan
7514
Yibin
Changde
Changsha
Wenzho

Guwahati
Myitkyina
Panzhihua
Lupanshui
Guiyang
Changsha
Hengyang
Fuzhou

INDIA
BANGLADESH
Dhaka

C H I N A

Kunming
Liuzhou
Xiamen

MYANMAR
(BURMA)

Mandalay
Nanning
Yulin
Guangzhou
Macau
Shantou
Gaoxiong

VIETNAM
Hanoi
Hai Phong
Zhanjiang
Hong Kong

Nay Pyi Taw
Louangphabang
Gulf of
Tongking
Haikou

Bay of
Bengal

LAOS
Hainan

Pegu
Chiang
Mai
Vientiane
Vinh

Bassein
Yangon

THAILAND

Da Nang

S o u t h

Lu

Andaman
Islands
(India)
Andaman
Sea

Nakhon
Ratchasima
Pakse

C h i n a

Quez
C
Mani

Mergui
Bangkok
Sisophon

CAMBODIA
Phnom
Penh

S e a

Gulf
of
Kâmpôt

Nha Trang

Nicobar Islands
(India)

Thailand
Cần Thơ
Ho Chi
Minh City

Palawan

Phuket
Nakhon Si
Thammarat

Su
Se

Banda
Aceh
George Town
Kota Bharu

Gunung
Kinabalu
4095
Sandak

M A L A Y S I A

Bandar Seri
Begawan
BRUNEI

Ipoh

Medan
Kuala Lumpur

Natuna
Besar

Strait of Malacca
Putrajaya
Sibu
Kuching

Nias
Singapore
SINGAPORE

B o r n e o

Sumatra
Pontianak
Samarinda
Balikpapan
Palu

Padang
Gunung
Kerinci
3805
Bangka

Macassar Strait
Cele

Kepulauan Mentawai
Bengkulu
Palembang
Banjarmasin

I N D I A N
Bandar Lampung
Java Sea
I N D O N

O C E A N
Jakarta
Bandung
Semarang
Makassar

Java
Surabaya
Flores

Bali
Sumbawa

38

East China
Sea

Ryukyu Islands

aipei

WAN

ait

P A C I F I C

O C E A N

Pagan

Northern
Mariana
Islands
(USA)

Saipan

Guam
(USA)

HILIPPINES

Samar

ay

os

Yap

FEDERATED STATES
OF MICRONESIA

Mindanao

Melekeok
PALAU

Davao

hipelago

es

Manado

Molucca Sea

Halmahera

Manokwari

Doberai
Peninsula

Jayapura

Bismarck Archipelago

Bismarck
Sea

Kepulauan
Sula

Seram

Ceram Sea

New

PAPUA

New Britain

Buru

Pegunungan Maoke

Puncak
Jaya
5030

Guinea

NEW

Solomon

Buton

Banda Sea

Kepulauan
Aru

GUINEA

Sea

I A

Kepulauan
Tanimbar

Dili

Gulf of
Papua

Port
Moresby

T TIMOR

EAST TIMOR

Arafura Sea

Torres Strait

Timor

KAZAKHSTAN

Lake Balkhash

Almaty

Bishkek

KYRGYZSTAN

Jengish Chokusu

7439

Tien Shan

Karamay

Ürümqi

Bohu

Tarim Basin

Taklimakan Shamo

K2
8611

Karakoram Range

Aksai Chin

Kunlun Shan

Altai Mountains

Hovd

Altay

MONGO

Ulan Bator

Kyakhta

Gobi Desert

Yumen

Golmud

Yinchuan

Xining

Lanzhou

Plateau of Tibet

Tianshui

Xi'an

Hanzhong

Himalaya

NEPAL

Kathmandu

Lucknow

Patna

Varanasi

Dhanbad

INDIA

Jamshedpur

Asansol

Kolkata

Mount Everest
8848

Kangchenjunga
8586

Thimphu

BHUTAN

BANGLADESH

Dhaka

Khulna

Nagqu

Lhasa

Dibrugarh

Guwahati

Myitkyina

Chengdu

Mianyang

Nanchong

Wanx

Leshan

Chongqing

Gongga Shan
7514

Yibin

Panzhihua

Lupanshui

Guiyang

Qujing

Kunming

Liuzhou

Cuttack

Mouths of the Ganges

Vishakhapatnam

Bay of Bengal

Nay Pyi Taw

MYANMAR (BURMA)

Mandalay

Pegu

Chiang Mai

THAILAND

Nanning

VIETNAM

Hanoi

Zhanjiang

Hai Phong

Louangphabang

LAOS

Vientiane

Vinh

Gulf of Tongking

Hainan

Haik

Y

Caspian
Sea

Elburz
Mountains

Gorgan

Ashgabat

TURKMENISTAN

Dushanbe

TAJIKISTAN

K2
8611

Karakoram Range

Mashhad

Mazar-e
Sharif

Hindu Kush

Tehran

Sabzevar

Qom

I R A N

Herat

Kabul

Peshawar

Srinagar

Isfahan

Yazd

Birjand

AFGHANISTAN

Rawalpindi

Islamabad

Gujranwala

Ahvaz

Zagros Mountains

Kerman

Kandahar

Lahore

Amritsar

Shiraz

Faisalabad

Ludhia

Zahedan

Quetta

Multan

Meerut
Delhi

The Gulf

Bandar-e 'Abbas

PAKISTAN

Thar Desert

New Delhi
Faridabad

BAHRAIN

Manama

QATAR

Dubai

Makran

Jaipur

Agra

Doha

OMAN

Jodhpur

Kota

Abu Dhabi

Gulf of Oman

Hyderabad

**UNITED ARAB
EMIRATES**

Muscat

Karachi

Bhopal

SAUDI ARABIA

Arabian
Peninsula

Ahmadabad

Vadodara

Indore

Rajkot

I

O M A N

Masirah

Surat
Nashik

Auranga

YEMEN

Arabian
Sea

Mumbai

Pune

D e c

Sola

Salalah

Western Ghats

Socotra
(Yemen)

Kur

Cape
Guardafui

Mangalore

Bangal

INDIAN OCEAN

Coimbatore

Kochi

Laccadive
Islands
(India)

Thiruvananthapuran

MALDIVES

42

un Shan

Plateau
of Tibet

C H I N A

Hanzhong

Jingmen

Mianyang · Wanxian

Chengdu · Nanchong

Changde

Nagqu

Leshan · Chongqing

Yibin

Gongga
Shan
7514

Guiyang

Lhasa

Panzhihua · Lupanshui

Qujing

Liuzhou

8091
Annapurna

Dibrugarh

a l a y a

Mount Everest

8848
Kangchenjunga

8586

Thimphu
BHUTAN

Guwahati

Myitkyina

Kunming

Nanning

NEPAL

reilly

cknow Kathmandu

Gorakhpur

Kanpur · Patna

Varanasi

ahabad

Dhanbad · Asansol

Jabalpur

Ranchi

Jamshedpur

Kolkata

BANGLADESH

Dhaka

Khulna

Chittagong

MYANMAR
(BURMA)

Mandalay

VIETNAM · Hanoi

Hai Phong

Gulf of
Tongking

LAOS

Louangphabang

Vinh

I A

agpur

Durg-
Bhilainagar

Eastern Ghats

Cuttack

Mouths
of the Ganges

Sittwe

Nay Pyi Taw

Pegu

Chiang
Mai

Vientiane

Pakxe

derabad

Vishakhapatnam

Bay
of
Bengal

Bassein

Yangon

THAILAND

Nakhon
Ratchasima

Vijayawada

Mergui

Bangkok

Sisophon

CAMBODIA

Phnom
Penh

Kâmpôt

Gulf
of
Thailand

Cǎn Thơ

Chennai

Andaman
Islands
(India)

Andaman
Sea

Nakhon Si
Thammarat

em

Phuket

Kota Bharu

adurai

Jaffna

Strait of Malacca

George
Town

MALAYSIA

SRI LANKA

Nicobar Islands
(India)

Ipoh

Kuala
Lumpur

olombo

Sri Jayewardenepura
Kotte

Banda Aceh

INDONESIA

Medan

Putrajaya

ASIA

Bay of Bengal

Yangon ⊡

Kolkata ○

Mumbai ○

Arabian Sea

Laccadive Is (India)

Andaman Is (India)

Nicobar Is (India)

Sri Lanka

Sri Jayewardenepura Kotte ⊡

Maldives

Chagos Archipelago (UK)

Socotra (Yemen)

INDIAN

Seychelles

The Gulf

Red Sea

AFRICA

Mogadishu ⊡

Dar es Salaam ○

Sumatra

Jakarta ⊡ Java

Java 7125

OCEANIA

Perth

O C E A N

SOUTHERN OCEAN

ANTARCTICA

Madagascar

Mauritius

Antananarivo

Réunion
(France)

Mozambique Channel

Îles Kerguelen
(France)

Îles Crozet
(France)

Maputo

Durban

Prince Edward Is
(S. Africa)

45

GREECE

Aegean
Sea

Patras

Athens

Izmir

Istanbul

Bursa

Black Sea

Samsun

Bat'umi

Sochi

RUSSIAN
FED.

Caucasus

Elbrus
5642

Grozznyy

Aktau

Ust
Pla

Makhachkala

GEORGIA

T'bilisi

Caspian

Bey

Konya

Kayseri

Erzurum

ARMENIA

Yerevan

Gäncä

AZERBAIJAN

AZER.

Baku

TU

Antalya

Adana

Taurus

Mts

Malatya

Mt Ararat
5165

Tabriz

Sea

Turkmenbe

TURKEY

Ankara

Crete

Rhodes

Nicosia

CYPRUS

Gaziantep

Lake
Van

Mesopotamia

Elburz

Mountains

Gorga

TU

Mediterranean Sea

Beirut

LEBANON

Homs

Aleppo

SYRIA

Mosul

Arbil

Kermanshah

Qom

Tehran

Alexandria

Tel Aviv-Yafo

ISRAEL

Jerusalem

GAZA

Damascus

Baghdad

IRAQ

Qattara
Depression

Cairo

Giza

Port Said

'Amman

Syrian

Desert

Isfahan

IRA

Al Fayyum

Suez

JORDAN

Yazd

Sinai

Aqaba

Al Jawf

Basra

Ahvaz

Zagros

Kerm

Asyut

Tabuk

KUWAIT

Kuwait

Shiraz

Mountain

EGYPT

Luxor

Al Qusayr

Hijaz

SAUDI ARABIA

The Gulf

Bandar-e
'Abbas

Aswan

Lake
Nasser

Medina

BAHRAIN

Manama

QATAR

Doha

Dubai

OM

Wadi Halfa

Riyadh

UNITED ARAB
EMIRATES

Abu Dha

Jeddah

Mecca

Arabian

Port Sudan

Atbara

SUDAN

Khartoum

Kassala

ERITREA

Asir

Abha

Peninsula

Rub' al Khali

OMAN

Red

Sea

Karora

Wad
Medani

Asmara

San'a

YEMEN

Salalah

Ras Dejen
4533

ETHIOPIA

Gonder

Aden

Mukalla

Lake
Tana

DJIBOUTI

Gulf of Aden

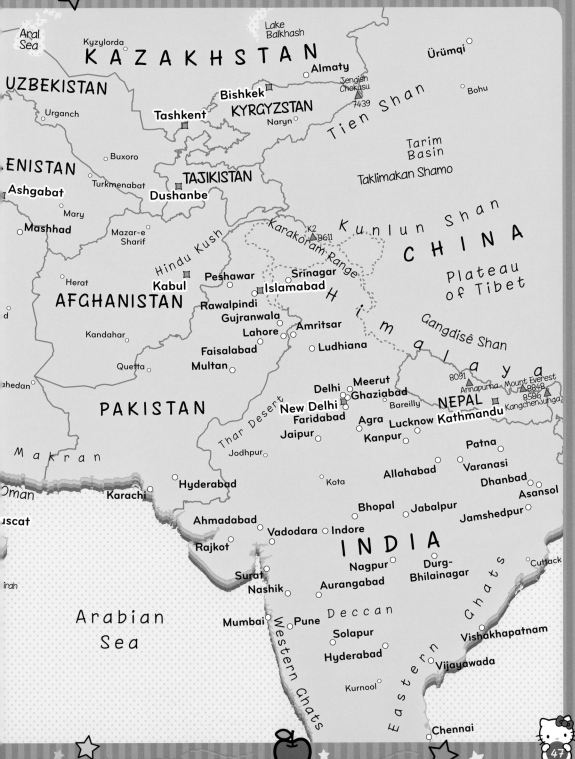

Aral Sea

Kyzylorda

K A Z A K H S T A N

Lake Balkhash

Ürümqi

Almaty

Bohu

UZBEKISTAN

Bishkek

Jengish Chokusu
7439

KYRGYZSTAN

Urganch

Tashkent

Naryn

Tien Shan

Buxoro

Tarim Basin

Taklimakan Shamo

ENISTAN

TAJIKISTAN

Ashgabat

Dushanbe

Mazar-e Sharif

Turkmenabat

Kunlun Shan

K2
8611

C H I N A

Mashhad

Mary

Karakoram Range

Plateau of Tibet

Herat

Hindu Kush

Peshawar

Srinagar

Kabul

Islamabad

H

d

Rawalpindi

Gujranwala

i

Gangdisê Shan

AFGHANISTAN

Lahore

Amritsar

m

Kandahar

Ludhiana

a

Faisalabad

l

8091
Annapurna

Mount Everest
8848

Quetta

Multan

Delhi

Meerut

a

Kangchenjunga
8586

ahedan

Thar Desert

Ghaziabad

Bareilly

NEPAL

y

a

PAKISTAN

New Delhi

Faridabad

Agra

Lucknow

Kathmandu

Jaipur

Kanpur

Jodhpur

Patna

Kota

Allahabad

Varanasi

Hyderabad

Dhanbad

Asansol

Oman

Karachi

Bhopal

Jabalpur

Jamshedpur

uscat

Ahmadabad

Indore

I N D I A

Cuttack

irah

Rajkot

Vadodara

Nagpur

Durg-Bhilainagar

Surat

Aurangabad

Deccan

Vishakhapatnam

Nashik

Eastern Ghats

Arabian Sea

Mumbai

Pune

Solapur

Vijayawada

Western Ghats

Hyderabad

Kurnool

Chennai

47

ICELAND

Norwegian Sea

Greenland Sea

A R C T I C

Spitsbergen
Svalbard (Norway)

Faroe Islands (Denmark)

UNITED KINGDOM

Aberdeen

North Sea

Bergen

Trondheim

Barents Sea

Zemlya Frantsa-Iosifa

N O R W A Y

Oslo

Copenhagen

Aalborg

Odense
Malmö

Gothenburg

S W E D E N

Stockholm

Gulf of Bothnia

Turku

FINLAND

Novaya Zemlya

Kara Sea

POLAND

Warsaw

LITHUANIA

LATVIA

Riga

ESTONIA

Tallinn

Helsinki

St Petersburg

Lake Ladoga

Petrozavodsk

Murmansk

Kola Peninsula

White Sea

Archangel

Yamal Peninsula

Obskaya Guba

Gydan Peninsula

Noril'sk

Brest

BELARUS

Vilnius

Minsk

Moscow

Smolensk

Yaroslavl'

Vorkuta

U r a l   M o u n t a i n s

R U S S I A N

Lviv

Kiev

UKRAINE

Tula

Kursk

Voronezh

Nizhniy Novgorod

Kazan'

Sarapul

Perm'

Serov

Surgut

Nizhnevartovsk

Syktyvkar

Chisinau

Kirovohrad

Odesa

Kharkiv

Saratov

Penza

Ul'yanovsk

Samara

Ufa
1153

Chelyabinsk

Yekaterinburg

Sea of Azov

Donets'k

Rostov-na-Donu

Volgograd

Orenburg

Omsk

Tomsk

Novosibirsk

Simferopol

Black Sea

Krasnodar

Elbrus 5642

GEORGIA

Grozny

Astrakhan'

Atyrau

Aktobe

Rudnyy

Astana

Pavlodar

Barnaul

TURKEY

ARMENIA

Tbilisi

Yerevan
5165

AZERBAIJAN

Baku

Caspian Sea

Karagandy

Semey

Altai Mountains

IRAQ

IRAN

Ustyurt Plateau

Aktau

Aral Sea

UZBEKISTAN

K A Z A K H S T A N

Lake Balkhash

Russian Federation

CEAN

Chukchi Sea

Bering Strait

Bering Sea

U.S.A.

maya
mlya

Vilkitskogo

Laptev Sea

New Siberia Islands

nyr Peninsula

Yukagirskoye
Ploskogor'ye

Kolymskoye Nagor'ye

Karaginskiy
Zaliv

3003
Khrebet Cherskogo

Verkhoyanskiy Khr.

2984

Magadan

Kamchatka
Peninsula

Sopka
Klyuchevskaya
3456

Petropavlovsk-
Kamchatskiy

S i b e r i a

Sea of
Okhotsk

Yakutsk

Central Siberian

Sakhalin

FEDERATION

Plateau

Stanovoy Khrebet

2482

Yuzhno-
Sakhalinsk

Ust'-
Ilimsk

2618

Bratsk

Blagoveshchensk

Khabarovsk

Sikhote-Alin'

Sapporo

rasnoyarsk

Lake
Baikal

Chita

Jiamusi

JAPAN

Sendai

Irkutsk

Ulan-
Ude

Qiqihar

Da Hinggan Ling

Harbin

Vladivostok

Akita

Daqing

C H I N A

Jilin

Ch'ongjin

Tokyo

Ulan Bator

Changchun

Fushun

NORTH KOREA

Nagoya

M O N G O L I A

Jan Mayen
(Norway)

ICELAND
Reykjavík

Atlantic
Ocean

Faroe Islands
(Denmark)

NORWAY

SWEDEN

FINLAND

Oslo

Stockholm

Helsinki

St Petersbu

Tallinn

ESTONIA

North
Sea

Edinburgh

Belfast

Dublin

IRELAND

UNITED
KINGDOM

London

DENMARK

Copenhagen

Baltic Sea

RUSSIA

Riga

LATVIA

LITHUANIA

Vilnius

Minsk

BELARUS

NETHERLANDS

Amsterdam

Berlin

Warsaw

POLAND

Brussels

GERMANY

BELGIUM

LUXEMBOURG

Prague

CZECH REPUBLIC

UKR

English Channel

Paris

SLOVAKIA

MOLDOVA

Munich

Vienna

Bratislava

Chisinau

Bay
of
Biscay

FRANCE

Bern

LIECHTENSTEIN

AUSTRIA

Budapest

SWITZERLAND

HUNGARY

ROMANIA

Lyon

SLOVENIA

Ljubljana

Zagreb

Belgrade

Bucharest

Milan

CROATIA

BOSNIA-
HERZEGOVINA

SERBIA

SAN
MARINO

Sarajevo

BULGARIA

PORTUGAL

ANDORRA

MONACO

ITALY

MONTENEGRO

Podgorica

KOSOVO

Sofia

Corsica

Rome

Tirana

Skopje

MACEDONIA

Istanbul

Lisbon

Madrid

Barcelona

SPAIN

Palma de
Mallorca

Sardinia

ALBANIA

Aegean

GREECE

Sea

Balearic
Islands

Mediterranean Sea

Gibraltar (UK)

Sicily

Athens

Crete

Rho

MALTA

50

The land area of Europe covers just over 2% of the world. It is the second smallest continent and extends far north into the Arctic Ocean and south to the Mediterranean Sea. In the north the winters are long and cold. In the south the weather is much warmer. Europe has over 40 countries and a wide variety of cultures, languages and religions.

RUSSIAN
FEDERATION

R. Volga

☐ Moscow

Volgograd

Caspian
Sea

El'brus △

lack
ea

TURKEY

Facts.

Area:
9 908 599 square kilometres
(3 825 731 square miles)

Largest country:
Ukraine
603 700 square kilometres
(233 090 square miles)
(excluding Russian Federation)

Longest river:
Volga
3 688 kilometres (2 292 miles)

Highest mountain:
El'brus
5 642 metres (18 510 feet)

Largest lake:
Caspian Sea
371 000 square kilometres
(143 243 square miles)

Largest island:
Great Britain
218 476 square kilometres
(84 354 square miles)

ICELAND

○ Akureyri

□ **Reykjavík**

○ Seyðhisfjörðhur

Norwegian
Sea

Trondheim ○

Öste...

ATLANTIC
OCEAN

Faroe
Islands
(Denmark)

Ålesund ○

Galdhøpiggen
▲
2470

N

Shetland
Islands

Bergen ○

Lillehammer ○

Oslo □

Outer Hebrides

Orkney
Islands

Drammen ○

Karlsta...

Vän...

○ Inverness

Ben
Nevis ▲
1344   Grampian Mts

○ Aberdeen

Stavanger ○

Vätt...

○ Stavanger

Glasgow

○ Dundee

N o r t h
S e a

Kristiansand ○

Gothenburg ○

Londonderry ○

○ Edinburgh

U N I T E D

Skagerrak

Ålborg ○

Kattegat

○ Belfast

Carlisle ○

K I N G D O M

Newcastle upon Tyne ○

DENMARK

Halm...

Galway ○

IRELAND

Blackpool ○
Irish Sea

○ Århus

Esbjerg ○

Copenhagen □

○ Limerick

Dublin

Leeds ○

Manchester ○

○ Odense

M...

○ Cork

Wexford ○

Liverpool
Sheffield ○

○ Kiel

Rosto...

Birmingham

Nottingham ○

Groningen ○

Hamburg

Swansea ○

Oxford ○

Norwich ○

NETHERLANDS

IJsselmeer

Bremen ○

G E R M A N Y

Cardiff ○

○ Bristol

London □

Amsterdam □

Hannover

Plymouth ○

Southampton ○

○ Dover

The Hague □
Rotterdam

Bielefeld

Ber...

Magdeburg ○

North Cape
Havøysund
Kirkenes
Tromsø
Murmansk

Barents Sea

vik

N
A
Y
Lappland

Kola Peninsula

Mezen'

Kandalaksha

White Sea

Archangel

Luleå
Oulu

Belomorsk

Syktyvkar

Umeå

Medvezh'yegorsk

Kotlas

Vaasa

FINLAND
Kuopio

Konosha

Gulf of Bothnia

Jyväskylä

Petrozavodsk
Lake Onega

Sundsvall

Lake Ladoga

Pori
Tampere

Cherepovets
Vologda

Turku
Vantaa
Helsinki

St Petersburg

Kostroma

Lahti

Velikiy Novgorod

Rybinsk Reservoir

ras

Gulf of Finland

Yaroslavl'

Stockholm
Hiiumaa
Tallinn

Lake Peipus

RUSSIAN

köping

ESTONIA
Pärnu

Pskov

Vladimir
Nizhniy Novgorod

Baltic Sea

Saaremaa
Gulf of Riga

Velikiye Luki

FEDERATION

Gotland

LATVIA

Moscow

Öland

Riga

Liepaja

Ryazan'

Daugavpils

nholm

Klaipeda
LITHUANIA

Smolensk

Tambov

Gdansk

RUSSIAN FED.
Kaliningrad
Kaunas

Orsha

Bryansk
Orel

Vilnius
Minsk

Mahilyow

Kursk
Voronezh
Borisoglebsk

cin

POLAND

Białystok

BELARUS

Baranavichy

Homyel'

Bydgoszcz

Poznan

Brest
Mazyr

Chernihiv
Sumy

Belgorod

UKRAINE

Warsaw

Shetland
Islands

Lerwick

Orkney
Islands

Kirkwall

Duncansby Head

Wick

Thurso

Cape Wrath

Ullapool

Stornoway

Isle of
Lewis

Tarbert

The Minch

Uig

Skye

Outer Hebrides

St Kilda

Moray Firth

Inverness

Loch
Ness

Cairngorm Mts

Ben Macdui
1309

Grampian Mountains

North West Highlands

Ben
Nevis

1344

Fort William

Oban

Ben More

1174

Loch
Lomond

Mull

Jura

Islay

Inner Hebrides

Aberdeen

Dundee

Perth

Stirling

Firth of Forth

Edinburgh

Berwick-upon-
Tweed

Scotland

Glasgow

ATLANTIC

OCEAN

Sea

North Sea

FRANCE

Norwich
Southend-on-Sea
Dover
Calais
Dieppe
King's Lynn
The Wash
Cambridge
Ipswich
Harwich
Le Havre
Kingston upon Hull
Grimsby
Scarborough
Peterborough
Watford
London
Ashford
Brighton
Eastbourne
Beachy Head
Cherbourg
Lincoln
Northampton
Oxford
Swindon
Reading
Southampton
Portsmouth
Isle of Wight
Sheffield
Nottingham
Coventry
Wolverhampton
Gloucester
Bristol
Bath
Salisbury
Bournemouth
Channel Islands
Perros-Guirec
Stoke-on-Trent
Chester
Hereford
Newport
Exeter
Weymouth
Granville
Shrewsbury
Birmingham
Brecon Beacons
Cardiff
Taunton
Dartmoor
Plymouth
England
Wales
Cambrian Mountains
Swansea
Pembroke
Bristol Channel
Snowdon 1085
Cardigan Bay
Aberystwyth
Fishguard
St David's Head
Penzance
Land's End
Isles of Scilly

Sunderland
Middlesbrough
Darlington
York
Leeds
Preston
Manchester
Liverpool
Blackpool
Carlisle
Lake District
Scafell Pike 977
Pennines
KINGDOM
Dumfries
Stranraer
Isle of Man
Douglas
Anglesey
Holyhead
Caernarfon
Wicklow
Irish Sea
St George's Channel

Southern Uplands
Larne
North Channel
Belfast
Newry
Slieve Donard 852
Dundalk
Drogheda
Dublin
Rosslare
Wexford
Waterford

Northern Ireland
Londonderry
Lough Neagh
Enniskillen
Lough Ree
Sligo
Donegal
Ballina
Westport
Galway
Lough Corrib
Lough Mask
Lough Derg
Limerick
Tralee
Dingle
Carrantuohill 1041
Cork

IRELAND

Celtic Sea

English Channel

55

ATLANTIC
OCEAN

IRELAND
Wexford
Cork

Nottingham Sheffield
Birmingham
Norwich
UNITED KINGDOM
Swansea Oxford
Cardiff
London
Bristol
Southampton
Plymouth
Channel Islands
Brest
Rennes
Nantes

NETHERLANDS Groningen Hamb
Amsterdam IJsselmeer Hanno
The Hague Bielefeld
Rotterdam
Dover Brugge Antwerp Essen
Calais Brussels Bonn Düsseldorf
Lille BELGIUM Cologne
Liège GERM
Luxembourg LUXEMBOURG
Frank
Reims
Nancy Karlsruh
Strasbourg Stuttga

English Channel
Le Havre Amiens
Caen Rouen
Paris
Le Mans
Tours Orléans

Bay La Rochelle
of
Biscay
Bordeaux

FRANCE
Poitiers
Dijon Basel
Zürich
Bern LIECHTENS
SWITZERLAND
Limoges Clermont-
Ferrand Lyon
Mont Blanc Geneva
4810
Massif
Central
Grenoble A
Milan
Turin

A Coruña
Vigo
Braga
Oporto
Coimbra
Lisbon
PORTUGAL

Gijón Santander Bayonne
Gulf
of Gascony
Cantabrian Mountains
León
Burgos
Valladolid
Salamanca
Madrid
Badajoz
Sierra Morena
Córdoba
Seville
Faro
Cádiz
Tangier
Tétouan
Rabat
Fez

Bilbao
Pamplona
Pyrenees
Aneto
3404
ANDORRA Andorra
la Vella
Zaragoza Barcelona

SPAIN

Toulouse Montpellier
Avignon Nice
Perpignan Monte
Marseille Carlo
MONACO

Genoa
Flore
Pisa

Corsica
Ajaccio

Valencia
Albacete
Alicante
Sierra Nevada
Málaga
Cartagena
Almería
Gibraltar (UK)
Strait of Gibraltar
Ceuta (Spain)

Palma de
Mallorca
Ibiza
Majorca
Balearic Islands
Minorca

Sassari
Sardinia
Cagliari

Granada

Algiers
Melilla
(Spain)
Oran
Ech Chélif
Constantine
Sétif

Annaba
Tu

Beni Mellal
MOROCCO
Oujda
Sidi Bel
Abbès
ALGERIA
Batna Tébessa
TUNISIA
So

Sfax

Rostock

Gdansk

Szczecin

Bydgoszcz

Białystok

Baranavichy

Minsk

Homyel'

Kursk

RUSSIAN FEDERATION

Belgorod

Berlin

Magdeburg

Poznan

Warsaw

Brest

BELARUS

Mazyr

Chernihiv

POLAND

Leipzig

Dresden

Łódz

Lublin

Rivne

Zhytomyr

Kiev

Kharkiv

Prague

Sudeten Mts

Wrocław

Kraków

L'viv

UKRAINE

Vinnytsya

Kirovohrad

Dnipropetrovs'k

Plzen

CZECH REPUBLIC

Ostrava

Khmel'nyts'kyy

Chernivtsi

Kryvyy Rih

Zaporizhzhya

emberg

Brno

SLOVAKIA

Kosice

Carpathian Mountains

Melitopol'

Vienna

Bratislava

Satu Mare

Pietrosa 2305

Balti

MOLDOVA

Chisinau

nich

Linz

AUSTRIA

Budapest

Debrecen

Bacau

Odesa

sbruck

Salzburg

Graz

HUNGARY

Cluj-Napoca

ROMANIA

Klagenfurt

Szeged

Sevastopol'

zano

SLOVENIA

Pécs

Timisoara

Brasov

Galati

Ljubljana

Zagreb

Novi Sad

Transylvanian Alps

Ploiesti

Bucharest

Constanta

Venice

Rijeka

CROATIA

Banja Luka

BOSNIA-HERZEGOVINA

Belgrade

Craiova

Ruse

Black Sea

San Marino

Split

SERBIA

Nió

Balkan Mts

Varna

Ancona

Sarajevo

Pristina

Sofia

Burgas

Zonguldak

Pescara

MONTENEGRO

Podgorica

Dubrovnik

KOSOVO

Plovdiv

BULGARIA

Edirne

Shkodër

Skopje

Istanbul

ne

Foggia

Tirana

ALBANIA

F.Y.R.O.M. MACEDONIA

Bitola

Gallipoli

Bursa

Ankara

Naples

Vesuvius 1281

Bari

Brindisi

Thessaloniki

Çanakkale

Izmir

Konya

enian

Mount Olympus 2911

Larisa

A e g e a n

TURKEY

a

Corfu

Ioannina

Pindus Mts

GREECE

S e a

Denizli

Antalya

Catanzaro

Patras

Athens

Izmir

almero

Mt Etna 3323

Reggio di Calabria

Corinth

Alanya

Sicily

Catania

Ionian Sea

Kalamata

Rhodes

Valletta

MALTA

Crete

Iraklion

a

n

e

a

n

S

e

a

EUROPE

AFRICA

NORTH AMERICA

ATLANTIC

Greenland
(Denmark)

Norwegian Sea

North Sea

London

British Isles

ICELAND

Bay of Biscay

Str. of Gibraltar

Rabat

Mediterranean Sea

Baffin Bay

Cape Farewell

Newfoundland

Azores (Port.)

Madeira (Port.)

Canary Islands (Spain)

CAPE VERDE ISLANDS

Ottawa

Washington D.C.

Hudson Bay

Bermuda (UK)

Sargasso Sea

THE BAHAMAS

Hispaniola

Milwaukee Deep 8605

Caribbean Sea

CUBA

Caracas

TRINIDAD

Gulf of
Guinea

Luanda

Cape
Town

Cape of
Good Hope

O C E A N

Ascension
Island
(UK)

St Helena
(UK)

Tristan
da Cunha
(UK)

Ilhas Martin Vas
(Brazil)

South
Georgia
(UK)

S O U T H

A M E R I C A

Rio de Janeiro

Buenos
Aires

Falkland Islands
(UK)

Tierra del Fuego

Cape Horn

PACIFIC
OCEAN

Azores
(Portugal)

Mediterranean Sea

Algiers

Tunis

Madeira
(Portugal)

Rabat

Casablanca

MOROCCO

TUNISIA

Tripoli

Benghazi

Alexandria

Cairo

Giza

Canary Is
(Spain)

Laayoune

WESTERN
SAHARA

ALGERIA

LIBYA

EGYPT

Sahara

Lake
Nasser

R. Nile

Red

MAURITANIA

Nouakchott

MALI

NIGER

CHAD

SUDAN

ERIT

Khartoum

Asma

CAPE VERDE

Praia

Dakar

SENEGAL

THE GAMBIA

GUINEA-BISSAU

Bamako

BURKINA
FASO

Niamey

Ouagadougou

Ndjamena

Conakry

GUINEA

SIERRA
LEONE

Freetown

CÔTE
D'IVOIRE

GHANA

TOGO

BENIN

NIGERIA

Abuja

CENTRAL
AFRICAN
REPUBLIC

SOUTH
SUDAN

Juba

Monrovia

LIBERIA

Yamoussoukro

Abidjan

Accra

Porto-Novo

Lagos

CAMEROON

Bangui

UGANDA

Kampala

KE

Na

Yaoundé

EQUATORIAL
GUINEA

Libreville

DEMOCRATIC

RWANDA

Lake
Victoria

SÃO TOMÉ &
PRINCIPE

GABON

CONGO

REPUBLIC

BURUNDI

Kilimanja

Brazzaville

OF THE

Dodoma

Kinshasa

CONGO

TANZAN

Atlantic
Ocean

Luanda

Ascension
Island
(UK)

ANGOLA

Lilongwe

MALAWI

ZAMBIA

St Helena (UK)

Lusaka

Harare

NAMIBIA

Windhoek

BOTSWANA

ZIMBABWE

Beira

MOZAMBIQ

Walvis Bay

Gaborone

Pretoria

Maputo

Johannesburg

SWAZILAND

Bloemfontein

LESOTHO

REPUBLIC OF
SOUTH AFRICA

Cape Town

Cape Agulhas

Africa is the second largest continent. It is 3 times the area of Europe. From the Mediterranean Sea in the north, Africa stretches approximately 8000 kilometres (4971 miles) to its most southerly point, Cape Agulhas. Most of northern Africa lies in and around the Sahara desert, while large areas of central Africa are covered in dense tropical rainforest.

DJIBOUTI
Djibouti

PIA

S O M A L I A

Mogadishu

mbasa

SEYCHELLES
Victoria

es Salaam

Aldabra Is
(Seychelles)

Maroni
COMOROS

Mayotte
(France)

Indian
Ocean

MADAGASCAR
Antananarivo

MAURITIUS
Reunion   Port
(France)   Louis

Facts.

Area:
Area: 30 343 578 square kilometres
(11 715 721 square miles)

Largest country:
Algeria
2 381 741 square kilometres
(919 595 square miles)

Longest river:
Nile
6695 kilometres (4160 miles)

Highest mountain:
Kilimanjaro
5892 metres (19 331 feet)

Largest lake:
Lake Victoria
68 800 square kilometres
(26 563 square miles)

Largest island:
Madagascar
587 040 square kilometres
(226 657 square miles)

Lyon

F R A N C E

Turin

A Coruña

Bayonne

MONACO

Bilbao

Pyrenees

Marseille

Oporto

S P A I N

ANDORRA

Corsica

Barcelona

Madrid

Valencia

Balearic Islands

Sardinia

A T L A N T I C

Lisbon

PORTUGAL

Majorca

O C E A N

Seville

Algiers

Annaba

M e d i t

Tangier

Ceuta
(Spain)

Oran

Constantine

Tunis

Melilla
(Spain)

Ech Chélif

Rabat

Fez

Oujda

Batna

Tébessa

TUNISIA

Casablanca

Madeira
(Portugal)

Béchar

Sfax

Marrakesh

Atlas Mountains

Jbel Toubkal
4167 ▲

Agadir

MOROCCO

Canary Is
(Spain)

A L G E R I A

Laâyoune

S a h a a

**WESTERN
SAHARA**

Mont Tahat
2918 ▲

Ahaggar

MAURITANIA

M A L I

Arlit

Mt Gréboun
1800 ▲

Massif
de l'Aïr

N I G E R

Tombouctou

Gao

SENEGAL Kayes

Mopti

Niamey

Zinder

ljana

SLOVENIA

Zagreb

CROATIA

NO

Belgrade

BOSNIA-
HERZEGOVINA

Sarajevo

SERBIA

ITALY

MONTENEGRO

Podgorica

KOSOVO

me

Bari

Tirana

MACEDONIA

ples

ALBANIA

Sofia

Skopje

BULGARIA

ROMANIA

Bucharest

Sevastopol'

Krasnodar

RUSSIAN
FED.

Caucasus

Black Sea

Sochi

GEORGIA

Thessaloniki

GREECE

Istanbul

Bursa

Ankara

TURKEY

ermo

Sicily

Athens

Izmir

Konya

Taurus Mountains

Aleppo

MALTA

Valletta

Crete

Antalya

Adana

SYRIA

bès

a

n e a n

S e a

Nicosia

CYPRUS

Beirut

LEBANON

Damascus

IRAQ

Tripoli

Gulf of
Sirte

Benghazi

Alexandria

Nile
Delta

ISRAEL

Tel Aviv-Yafo

Jerusalem

'Amman

JORDAN

Cairo

Giza

Qattara
Depression

Sinai

SAUDI
ARABIA

LIBYA

a

Libyan Desert

EGYPT

Asyut

Luxor

Hijaz

Red Sea

Tibesti

Aswan

Lake Nasser

Wadi Halfa

Jeddah

Mecca

au

do

Emi Koussi
3415

Nubian
Desert

Port
Sudan

CHAD

SUDAN

ERITREA

Asmara

Omdurman

Khartoum

Darfur

Lake Chad

El Obeid

Wad
Medani

Ras Dejen
4533

MOROCCO

Canary Is
(Spain)

Laâyoune

WESTERN
SAHARA

ATLANTIC

OCEAN

Nouâdhibou

MAURITANIA

Nouakchott

Santo
Antão

Boa
Vista

CAPE
VERDE

Fogo

Praia

Santiago

Dakar

SENEGAL

Kaolack

Kayes

Banjul

THE
GAMBIA

Bamak

GUINEA-
BISSAU

Bissau

Fouta
Djallon

GUINEA

Conakry

CÔT
D'IVO

Freetown

SIERRA
LEONE

LIBERIA

Yamoussou

Monrovia

Cape Palmas

ALGERIA

LIBYA

S a h a r a

Mont Tahat
2918 ▲

Ahaggar

Plateau
du Djado

MALI

Arlit ○

Mt Gréboun
1800 ▲

bouctou ○

Gao ○

Massif
de l'Aïr

NIGER

Mopti ○

CHAD

Zinder ○

Niamey ▣

Lake Chad

Ouagadougou ▣

Kano ○

Maiduguri ○

Ndjamena ▣

BURKINA FASO

NIGERIA

Abuja ▣ Jos
Plateau

GHANA

BENIN

TOGO

Lake Volta

Porto-
Novo ▣

Ibadan ○

Adamawa
Highlands

Ngaoundéré ○

Lomé ▣

Lagos ○

Benin
City ○

Enugu ○

djan

Accra ▣

Bight of
Benin

Port
Harcourt ○

CAMEROON

CENTRAL
AFRICAN
REPUBLIC

Mt Cameroun
4100 ▲

Douala ▣

Yaoundé ▣

Malabo ▣

Gulf of Guinea

EQUATORIAL
GUINEA

Mont Tahat ▲
2918

Ahaggar

ALGERIA

Plateau
du Djado

Tibesti

LIBYA

MALI

NIGER

CHAD

Darfur

● **Niamey**

● Zinder

Lake Chad

Jebel Marra ▲
3088

Kano ●

Maiduguri ●

■ **Ndjamena**

NIGERIA

Abuja ■

Jos
Plateau

Sarh ●

**CENTRAL
AFRICAN
REPUBLIC**

TOGO

BENIN

**Porto-
Novo** ■

● **Ibadan**

Lagos ●

**Benin
City** ●

Enugu ○

*Adamawa
Highlands*

Ngaoundéré ●

Lomé ■

Bight of
Benin

**Port
Harcourt** ●

CAMEROON

Mt Cameroun
4100 ▲

Douala ■

Bangui ■

Gulf of
Guinea

Malabo ■

Yaoundé ■

**EQUATORIAL
GUINEA**

**SÃO TOMÉ
AND PRÍNCIPE**

■ **Libreville**

CONGO

Kisangani ●

Mbandaka ○

**DEMOCRATIC
REPUBLIC
OF THE
CONGO**

Port-Gentil ●

GABON

Franceville ●

Congo
Basin

ATLANTIC

Brazzaville ■

Ilebo ○

Pointe-Noire ●
ANGOLA

■ **Kinshasa**

OCEAN

ANGOLA

Kananga ●

EGYPT

Wadi Halfa

Red Sea

Jeddah
Mecca

SAUDI
ARABIA

'Asir

Rub' al Khali

OMAN

Nubian
Desert

Port
Sudan

SUDAN

San'a

YEMEN

Omdurman

Khartoum

ERITREA

Asmara

Wad
Medani

El Obeid

Ras Dejen
△
4533

Lake Tana

Aden

Gulf of Aden

Socotra
Hajhir △
1503

DJIBOUTI

Djibouti

Berbera

Vau

Ethiopian
Highlands

Dire
Dawa

Addis Ababa

SOUTH
SUDAN

ETHIOPIA

SOMALIA

Sudd

Juba

Lake Albert

UGANDA

Lake Turkana

KENYA

Mogadishu

Margherita
Peak
5110 △

Kampala

Kisumu

Mount Kenya
△
5199

Lake
ward

Lake
Victoria

Nairobi

Kismaayo

INDIAN

ANDA

Kigali

Mwanza

Kilimanjaro
△
5892

avu

Bujumbura

Arusha

OCEAN

BURUNDI

Kigoma

Mombasa

Pemba Island

TANZANIA

Tanga

Dodoma

Zanzibar
Zanzibar Island

Lake
Tanganyika

Dar es Salaam

67

Brazzaville
Pointe-Noire
ANGOLA
Kinshasa
Ilebo
Kananga

DEMOCRATIC
REPUBLIC
OF THE
CONGO

Kigome

Lake
Tanganyika

Luanda

Malanje

Lake Mweru

Kolwezi
Likasi

Lubumbashi

ANGOLA

Benguela

Huambo

Bié
Plateau

Kitwe
Ndola

Namibe
Lubango

ZAMBIA

Lusaka

Lake Kariba

Livingstone
Victoria
Falls

Harare

Matabele
Upland

Etosha
Pan

ZIMBABW

NAMIBIA

Bulawayo

Namib Desert

BOTSWANA

Kalahari
Desert

Walvis Bay
Windhoek

Gaborone

Pretoria
Maputo

Johannesburg
Mbabane
Soweto
SWAZILAND

Lüderitz

REPUBLIC OF

ATLANTIC

Bloemfontein
LESOTHO
Maseru

Drakensberg
Pietermaritzb

OCEAN

SOUTH AFRICA

Durba

Great Karoo

East London

Cape Town

Cape of Good Hope

Port Elizabeth

Cape Agulhas

Mombasa

Tanga

Pemba Island

Dodoma ◻

Zanzibar
Zanzibar Island

Dar es Salaam

TANZANIA

Mbeya

Mafia Island

Aldabra
Islands

Lake Nyasa

Mtwara

Maroni
◻ COMOROS

Mayotte
(Fr.)

MALAWI

Lichinga

◻ **Lilongwe**

Nacala

ntyre

Nampula

Mahajanga

MOZAMBIQUE

Mozambique Channel

Beira

Toamasina

◻ **Antananarivo**

MADAGASCAR

Fianarantsoa

Port Louis ◻ MAURITIUS

Réunion
(Fr.)

Mahé ▪ SEYCHELLES

INDIAN

OCEAN

Cargados
Carajos Islands

South Orkney Is.

South Shetland Is.

Graham
Land

Antarctic
Peninsula

Weddell
Sea

Queen Maud Land

Ende

Palmer
Land

Berkner I.

Alexander I.

ANTARCTICA

▶ South
Pole

Bellingshausen
Sea

△ Vinson
Massif

Ellsworth
Land

Transantarctic Mountains

SOUTHERN OCEAN

Amundsen
Sea

Marie Byrd Land

Ross
Ice
Shelf

Ross
Sea

Oates
Land

Antarctica is an area of thick ice surrounding the South Pole. It is the coldest, windiest and driest continent. Very few plants and animals can survive here. Penguins, whales and seals live in and around Antarctica.

Kemp Land

Prydz Bay

S O U T H E R N   O C E A N

Queen Mary Land

Wilkes Land

Facts.

Area:
14 000 000 square kilometres (5 400 000 square miles)

Largest country:
There are no countries in Antarctica. The only people who live there are visiting scientists.

Highest mountain:
Vinson Massif
4892 metres (16 050 feet)

Ice:

The ice on Antarctica stores around 70% of the world's fresh water.

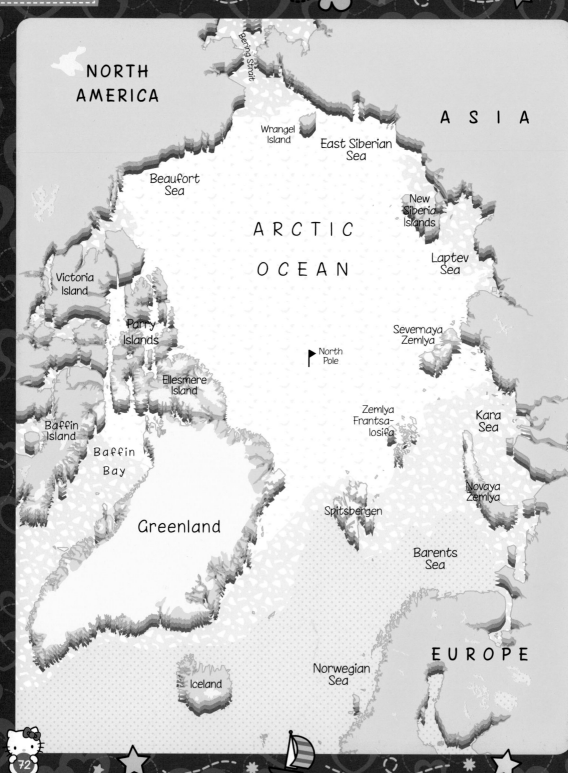

NORTH AMERICA

ASIA

Bering Strait

Wrangel Island

East Siberian Sea

Beaufort Sea

New Siberia Islands

ARCTIC

OCEAN

Laptev Sea

Victoria Island

Parry Islands

Severnaya Zemlya

North Pole

Ellesmere Island

Zemlya Frantsa-Iosifa

Kara Sea

Baffin Island

Baffin Bay

Novaya Zemlya

Greenland

Spitsbergen

Barents Sea

EUROPE

Iceland

Norwegian Sea

HELLO KITTY

World Atlas

Amazing Facts

Country Facts
and Flags

The Arctic Ocean is the smallest and shallowest ocean in the world

Lake Superior, one of the 5 Great Lakes, is North America's largest lake

NORTH AMERICA

The largest ocean in the world is the Pacific Ocean

The Amazon has the largest river drainage basin in the world

SOUTH AMERICA

The coast of Chile has more than 5 000 islands

EUROPE

The Caspian Sea is actually a lake. It is the largest lake in the world.

ASIA

The 100 highest mountains in the world are found in Asia

The longest river in Africa and the World is the Nile

The bottom of the Mariana Trench in the Pacific Ocean is the deepest place in the world

AFRICA

Victoria Falls has the widest falling sheet of water on the planet

Indonesia is made up of more than 13 000 separate islands

OCEANIA

Lake Eyre is the largest lake in Oceania, but it completely dries up in the summer

At its thickest, Antarctica's ice is more than 4 km thick

NORTH
AMERICA

Canada's coastline is over
200 000 km long

Hot chocolate was
introduced to Europeans
by an Aztec emperor

SOUTH
AMERICA

Earth is the only planet
in the solar system not
named after a Greek or
Roman god

76

EUROPE

The world's longest railway, the Trans Siberian Railway, runs from Moscow to Vladivostock

Switzerland has the world's highest per capita rate of chocolate consumption

ASIA

An oil well off Sakhalin island in Russia is the deepest hole ever dug

More people speak English in China than in the USA

AFRICA

The world's tallest building is Burj Khalifa in Dubai

When put together, China, Europe and the USA could fit inside the land area of Africa

The Danyang-Kunshan Grand Bridge on the Beijing to Shanghai Railway is the world's longest

16 countries in Africa have no coastline

OCEANIA

HELLO KITTY
SAFARI TOURS

Cities occupy less than 2 per cent of the Earth's land surface but house half of the human population

77

The greatest annual snowfall of over 31 000 mm occurred at Mt Rainier, Washington, USA between 1971 and 1972

NORTH AMERICA

An avalanche in Peru in 1970 killed more than 20 000 people

The Atacama Desert in Chile is the driest place on earth with an average of 0.1 mm of rain each year

SOUTH AMERICA

The largest recorded earthquake in the world was a magnitude 9.5 (MM) in Chile on May 22, 1960

A heatwave in Europe in 2003 killed 70 000 people

ASIA

ROPE

The world's deadliest recorded earthquake occurred in 1556 in central China, killing an estimated 830 000 people

The Iranian blizzard of February 1972 resulted in the deaths of approximately 4 000 people

AFRICA

The eruption of the volcano Krakatoa in 1883 could be heard 4 800 km away

OCEANIA

About 20 per cent of all volcanoes are under water

Country name
Capital city
Population
Area

 Angola
Luanda
19 618 000
1 246 700 sq km

 Afghanistan
Kabul
32 358 000
652 225 sq km

 Antigua and Barbuda
St John's
90 000
442 sq km

 Albania
Tirana
3 216 000
28 748 sq km

 Argentina
Buenos Aires
40 765 000
2 766 889 sq km

 Algeria
Algiers
35 980 000
2 381 741 sq km

 Armenia
Yerevan
3 100 000
29 800 sq km

 Andorra
Andorra la Vella
86 000
465 sq km

 Australia
Canberra
22 606 000
7 692 024 sq km

Austria
Vienna
8 413 000
83 855 sq km

 Barbados
Bridgetown
274 000
430 sq km

 Azerbaijan
Baku
9 306 000
86 600 sq km

 Belarus
Minsk
9 559 000
207 600 sq km

 The Bahamas
Nassau
347 000
13 939 sq km

 Belgium
Brussels
10 754 000
30 520 sq km

 Bahrain
Al Manamah
1 324 000
691 sq km

 Belize
Belmopan
318 000
22 965 sq km

 Bangladesh
Dhaka (Dacca)
150 494 000
143 998 sq km

 Benin
Porto-Novo
9 100 000
112 620 sq km

Bhutan
Thimphu
738 000
46 620 sq km

 Brunei
Bandar Seri Begawan
406 000
5 765 sq km

 Bolivia
La Paz/Sucre
10 088 000
1 098 581 sq km

 Bulgaria
Sofia
7 446 000
110 994 sq km

 Bosnia and Herzegovina
Sarajevo
3 752 000
51 130 sq km

 Burkina Faso
Ouagadougou
16 968 000
274 200 sq km

 Botswana
Gaborone
2 031 000
581 370 sq km

 Burundi
Bujumbura
8 575 000
27 835 sq km

 Brazil
Brasília
196 655 000
8 514 879 sq km

 Côte d'Ivoire
Yamoussoukro
20 153 000
322 463 sq km

Cambodia
Phnom Penh
14 305 000
181 035 sq km

Chad
Ndjamena
11 525 000
1 284 000 sq km

Cameroon
Yaoundé
20 030 000
475 442 sq km

Chile
Santiago
17 270 000
756 945 sq km

Canada
Ottawa
34 350 000
9 984 670 sq km

China
Beijing
1 332 079 000
9 584 492 sq km

Cape Verde
Praia
501 000
4 033 sq km

Colombia
Bogotá
46 927 000
1 141 748 sq km

Central African Republic
Bangui
4 487 000
622 436 sq km

Comoros
Moroni
754 000
1 862 sq km

Congo
Brazzaville
4 140 000
342 000 sq km

 Cyprus
Nicosia
1 117 000
9 251 sq km

 Congo, Democratic Republic of the
Kinshasa
67 758 000
2 345 410 sq km

 Czech Republic
Prague
10 534 000
78 864 sq km

 Costa Rica
San José
4 727 000
51 100 sq km

 Denmark
Copenhagen
5 573 000
43 075 sq km

 Croatia
Zagreb
4 396 000
56 538 sq km

 Djibouti
Djibouti
906 000
23 200 sq km

 Cuba
Havana
11 254 000
110 860 sq km

 Dominica
Roseau
68 000
750 sq km

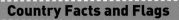

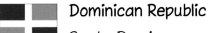
Dominican Republic
Santo Domingo
10 056 000
48 442 sq km

Equatorial Guinea
Malabo
720 000
28 051 sq km

East Timor
Dili
1 154 000
14 874 sq km

Eritrea
Asmara
5 415 000
117 400 sq km

Ecuador
Quito
14 666 000
272 045 sq km

Estonia
Tallinn
1 341 000
45 200 sq km

Egypt
Cairo
82 537 000
1 001 450 sq km

Ethiopia
Addis Ababa
84 734 000
1 133 880 sq km

El Salvador
San Salvador
6 227 000
21 041 sq km

Fiji
Suva
868 000
18 330 sq km

Finland
Helsinki
5 385 000
338 145 sq km

 Germany
Berlin
82 163 000
357 022 sq km

 France
Paris
63 126 000
543 965 sq km

 Ghana
Accra
24 966 000
238 537 sq km

 Gabon
Libreville
1 534 000
267 667 sq km

 Greece
Athens
11 390 000
131 957 sq km

 The Gambia
Banjul
1 776 000
11 295 sq km

 Grenada
St George's
105 000
378 sq km

 Georgia
Tbilisi
4 329 000
69 700 sq km

 Guatemala
Guatemala City
14 757 000
108 890 sq km

Guinea
Conakry
10 222 000
245 857 sq km

 Hungary
Budapest
9 966 000
93 030 sq km

 Guinea-Bissau
Bissau
1 547 000
36 125 sq km

 Iceland
Reykjavik
324 000
102 820 sq km

 Guyana
Georgetown
756 000
214 969 sq km

 India
New Delhi
1241 492 000
3 064 898 sq km

 Haiti
Port-au-Prince
10 124 000
27 750 sq km

 Indonesia
Jakarta
242 326 000
1 919 445 sq km

 Honduras
Tegucigalpa
7 755 000
112 088 sq km

 Iran
Tehran
74 799 000
1 648 000 sq km

Iraq
Baghdad
32 665 000
438 317 sq km

 Japan
Tokyo
126 497 000
377 727 sq km

 Ireland
Dublin
4 526 000
70 282 sq km

 Jordan
Amman
6 330 000
89 206 sq km

 Israel
Jerusalem
7 562 000
22 072 sq km

 Kazakhstan
Astana
16 207 000
2 717 300 sq km

 Italy
Rome
60 789 000
301 245 sq km

 Kenya
Nairobi
41 610 000
582 646 sq km

 Jamaica
Kingston
2 751 000
10 991 sq km

 Kiribati
Bairiki
101 000
717 sq km

Kosovo
Pristina
2 180 686
10 908 sq km

 Lebanon
Beirut
4 259 000
10 452 sq km

 Kuwait
Kuwait
2 818 000
17 818 sq km

 Lesotho
Maseru
2 194 000
30 355 sq km

 Kyrgyzstan
Bishkek
5 393 000
198 500 sq km

 Liberia
Monrovia
4 129 000
111 369 sq km

 Laos
Vientiane
6 288 000
236 800 sq km

Libya
Tripoli
6 423 000
1 759 540 sq km

 Latvia
Riga
2 243 000
64 589 sq km

 Liechtenstein
Vaduz
36 000
160 sq km

Lithuania
Vilnius
3 307 000
65 200 sq km

 Malaysia
Kuala Lumpur/
Putrajaya
28 859 000
332 965 sq km

 Luxembourg
Luxembourg
516 000
2 586 sq km

 Maldives
Male
320 000
298 sq km

 Macedonia (F.Y.R.O.M.)
Skopje
2 064 000
25 713 sq km
F.Y.R.O.M – Former Yugoslav
Republic of Macedonia

 Mali
Bamako
15 840 000
1 240 140 sq km

 Madagascar
Antananarivo
21 315 000
587 041 sq km

 Malta
Valletta
418 000
316 sq km

 Malawi
Lilongwe
15 381 000
118 484 sq km

 Marshall Islands
Delap-Uliga-Djarrit
55 000
181 sq km

Mauritania
Nouakchott
3 542 000
1 030 700 sq km

 Monaco
Monaco-Ville
35 000
2 sq km

 Mauritius
Port Louis
1 307 000
2 040 sq km

 Mongolia
Ulan Bator
2 800 000
1 565 000 sq km

 Mexico
Mexico City
114 793 000
1 972 545 sq km

 Montenegro
Podgorica
632 000
13 812 sq km

Micronesia, Federated States of
Palikir
112 000
701 sq km

 Morocco
Rabat
32 273 000
446 550 sq km

 Moldova
Chisinau
3 545 000
33 700 sq km

 Mozambique
Maputo
23 930 000
799 380 sq km

Myanmar (Burma)
Nay Pyi Taw
48 337 000
676 577 sq km

 New Zealand
Wellington
4 415 000
270 534 sq km

 Namibia
Windhoek
2 324 000
824 292 sq km

 Nicaragua
Managua
5 870 000
130 000 sq km

 Nauru
Yaren
10 000
21 sq km

 Niger
Niamey
16 069 000
1 267 000 sq km

 Nepal
Kathmandu
30 486 000
147 181 sq km

 Nigeria
Abuja
162 471 000
923 768 sq km

 Netherlands
Amsterdam/The Hague
16 665 000
41 526 sq km

 North Korea
Pyongyang
24 451 000
120 538 sq km

Norway
Oslo
4 925 000
323 878 sq km

 Papua New Guinea
Port Moresby
7 014 000
462 840 sq km

 Oman
Muscat
2 846 000
309 500 sq km

 Paraguay
Asunción
6 568 000
406 752 sq km

 Pakistan
Islamabad
176 745 000
803 940 sq km

 Peru
Lima
29 400 000
1 285 216 sq km

 Palau
Melekeok
21 000
497 sq km

 Philippines
Manila
94 852 000
300 000 sq km

 Panama
Panama City
3 571 000
77 082 sq km

 Poland
Warsaw
38 299 000
312 683 sq km

Portugal
Lisbon
10 690 000
88 940 sq km

 São Tomé and Príncipe
São Tomé
169 000
964 sq km

 Qatar
Doha
1 870 000
11 437 sq km

 Samoa
Apia
184 000
2 831 sq km

 Romania
Bucharest
21 436 000
237 500 sq km

 San Marino
San Marino
32 000
61 sq km

 Russian Federation
Moscow
142 836 000
17 075 400 sq km

 Saudi Arabia
Riyadh
28 083 000
2 200 000 sq km

 Rwanda
Kigali
10 943 000
26 338 sq km

 Senegal
Dakar
12 768 000
196 720 sq km

Serbia
Belgrade
7 306 677
77 453 sq km

 Slovenia
Ljubljana
2 035 000
20 251 sq km

 Seychelles
Victoria
87 000
455 sq km

 Solomon Islands
Honiara
552 000
28 370 sq km

 Sierra Leone
Freetown
5 997 000
71 740 sq km

 Somalia
Mogadishu
9 557 000
637 657 sq km

 Singapore
Singapore
5 188 000
639 sq km

 South Africa
Pretoria/Cape Town/
Bloemfontein
50 460 000
1 219 090 sq km

 Slovakia
Bratislava
5 472 000
49 035 sq km

 South Korea
Seoul
48 391 000
99 274 sq km

South Sudan
Juba
8 260 490
644 329 sq km

St Vincent and the Grenadines
Kingstown
109 000
389 sq km

Spain
Madrid
46 455 000
504 782 sq km

Sudan
Khartoum
36 371 510
1 861 484 sq km

Sri Lanka
Sri Jayewardenepura Kotte
21 045 000
65 610 sq km

Suriname
Paramaribo
529 000
163 820 sq km

St Kitts and Nevis
Basseterre
53 000
261 sq km

Swaziland
Mbabane
1 203 000
17 364 sq km

St Lucia
Castries
176 000
616 sq km

Sweden
Stockholm
9 441 000
449 964 sq km

Switzerland
Bern
7 702 000
41 293 sq km

Togo
Lomé
6 155 000
56 785 sq km

Syria
Damascus
20 766 000
184 026 sq km

Tonga
Nuku'alofa
105 000
748 sq km

Tajikistan
Dushanbe
6 977 000
143 100 sq km

Trinidad and Tobago
Port of Spain
1 346 000
5 130 sq km

Tanzania
Dodoma
46 218 000
945 087 sq km

Tunisia
Tunis
10 594 000
164 150 sq km

Thailand
Bangkok
69 519 000
513 115 sq km

Turkey
Ankara
73 640 000
779 452 sq km

Turkmenistan
Ashkhabad
5 105 000
488 100 sq km

 United Kingdom
London
62 417 000
243 609 sq km

 Uganda
Kampala
34 509 000
241 038 sq km

 United States of America
Washington D.C.
313 085 000
9 826 635 sq km

 Tuvalu
Vaiaku
10 000
25 sq km

 Uruguay
Montevideo
3 380 000
176 215 sq km

 Ukraine
Kiev
45 190 000
603 700 sq km

 Uzbekistan
Tashkent
27 760 000
447 400 sq km

 United Arab Emirates
Abu Dhabi
7 891 000
77 700 sq km

 Vanuatu
Port Vila
246 000
12 190 sq km

Vatican City
Vatican City
800
0.5 sq km

Zimbabwe
Harare
12 754 000
390 759 sq km

Venezuela
Caracas
29 437 000
912 050 sq km

Vietnam
Hanoi
88 792 000
329 565 sq km

Yemen
Șan'ā'
24 800 000
527 968 sq km

Zambia
Lusaka
13 475 000
752 614 sq km

A B C D E F G H I J K L M N O P Q R S T U V W X Y Z

A B C D E F G H I J K L M N O P Q R S T U V W X Y Z

A
B
C
D
E
F
G
H
I
J
K
L
M
N
O
P
Q
R
S
T
U
V
W
X
Y
Z

A
B
C
D
E
F
G
H
I
J
K
L
M
N
O
P
Q
R
S
T
U
V
W
X
Y
Z

A B C D E F G H I J K L M N O P Q R S T U V W X Y Z

A
B
C
D
E
F
G
H
I
J
K
L
M
N
O
P
Q
R
S
T
U
V
W
X
Y
Z

Linz 57
Lisbon 56
Lithuania 50
Little Rock 17
Liuzhou 40
Liverpool 55
Livingstone 68
Ljubljana 57
Łódz 57
Lofoten Islands 52
Lombok 38
Lomé 65
Lomond, Loch 54
London 55
Londonderry 55
Long Island
   (The Bahamas) 20
Long Island (U.S.A.) 17
Longlac 17
Los Angeles 16
Los Mochis 18
Louangphabang 38
Luanda 68
Lubango 68
Lubbock 16
Lublin 57
Lubumbashi 68
Lucknow 43
Lüderitz 68
Ludhiana 42
Luleå 53
Luoyang 41
Lupanshui 40
Lusaka 68
Luxembourg 50
Luxor 63
Luzon 38
Luzon Strait 38
L'viv 57
Lyon 56

M
Macapá 25
Macassar Strait 38
Macau 41
Macdonnell Ranges 30
Macedonia 50
Maceió 25
Machala 24
Madagascar 61
Madeira 62

Madison 17
Madrid 56
Madurai 43
Mafia Island 69
Magadan 49
Magdeburg 57
Magellan, Strait of 27
Mahajanga 69
Mahé 69
Mahilyow 53
Maiduguri 65
Majorca 56
Makassar 38
Makhachkala 46
Makran 42
Malabo 66
Malacca, Strait of 38
Málaga 56
Malanje 68
Malatya 46
Malawi 60
Malaysia 36
Maldives 36
Mali 60
Malmö 52
Malta 50
Manacapuru 24
Manado 39
Managua 19
Manama 46
Manaus 24
Manchester 55
Mandalay 43
Mangalore 42
Manila 38
Manizales 24
Manokwari 39
Manukau 32
Manzhouli 41
Maputo 68
Maquette 17
Mar del Plata 27
Maraba 25
Maracaibo 24
Maracay 24
Margherita Peak 67
Mariana Islands 9
Maria van Diemen,
   Cape 32
Marie Byrd Land 70
Maringá 26

Maroni 69
Marquesas Islands 35
Marrakesh 62
Marseille 56
Marshall Islands 34
Martinique 21
Mary 47
Maryborough 31
Maseru 68
Mashhad 47
Masirah 42
Massif Central 56
Massif de l'Aïr 65
Matabele Upland 68
Matagami 17
Matanzas 20
Maturin 24
Mauritania 60
Mauritius 61
Mayotte 69
Mazar-e Sharif 47
Mazatán 18
Mazyr 53
Mbabane 68
Mbandaka 66
Mbeya 69
McKinley, Mount 12
Mecca 46
Medan 38
Medellin 24
Medina 46
Mediterranean Sea 56
Medvezh'yegorsk 53
Meerut 42
Melanesia 34
Melbourne 31
Melekeok 39
Melilla 62
Melitopol' 57
Memphis 17
Mendoza 27
Mergui 38
Mérida 19
Mesopotamia 46
Mexicali 18
Mexico 12
Mexico City 18
Mexico, Gulf of 19
Mezen' 53
Miami 17
Mianyang 40

Michigan, Lake 17
Micronesia 34
Middlesbrough 55
Miguel 20
Milan 56
Miles City 16
Milwaukee 17
Milwaukee Deep 58
Minch, The 54
Mindanao 39
Mindoro 38
Minneapolis-St Paul 17
Minorca 56
Minot 16
Minsk 53
Mississippi Delta 17
Mississippi, River 12
Missouri, River 12
Mobile 17
Mogadishu 67
Moldova 50
Molucca Sea 39
Mombasa 67
Monaco 56
Monclova 18
Moncton 15
Mongolia 36
Monrovia 60
Monte Carlo 56
Montego Bay 20
Montenegro 50
Monterrey 18
Montes Claros 25
Montevideo 27
Montgomery 17
Montpelier 17
Montpellier 56
Montréal 15
Montserrat 21
Moosonee 17
Mopti 65
Moray Firth 54
Morgan City 17
Morocco 60
Moscow 48
Mosul 46
Mozambique 60
Mozambique Channel
   69
Mtwara 69
Mukalla 46

A B C D E F G H I J K L M N O P Q R S T U V W X Y Z

A
B
C
D
E
F
G
H
I
J
K
L
M
N
O
P
Q
R
S
T
U
V
W
X
Y
Z

A
B
C
D
E
F
G
H
I
J
K
L
M
N
O
P
Q
R

S
T
U
V
W
X
Y
Z

A
B
C
D
E
F
G
H
I
J
K
L
M
N
O
P
Q
R

S
T
U
V
W
X
Y
Z

A
B
C
D
E
F
G
H
I
J
K
L
M
N
O
P
Q
R
S
T
U
V
W
X
Y
Z